HOW CANCER SAVED MY LIFE

I Spy God!

HOW CANCER SAVED MY LIFE

I spy God!

Mary Jane Warr

Copyright © 2004 by Mary Jane Warr

No part of this book may be reproduced or transmitted in any form or by any means, electronic or mechanical, including photocopying and recording, or by any information storage or retrieval system without written permission from the author, except for brief passages quoted in a review.

Canadian Cataloguing in Publication Data

ISBN 09699506-2-4

Cover design by Susan Mellor

Other books by Mary Jane Warr

Making Sense of Your Fear of Flying, an awareness handbook for people who fear flying, 1997

Making Sense of Self-Esteem, 2008

Making Sense of Depression – Finding the Golden Key, 2010

Making Sense of Being Assertive – What to say and when to say it, 2011

All of Mary Jane Warr's books are published by Making Sense Books, Nanaimo, BC., and are available through our website:

www.makingsensebooks.ca

For Ruth,

my special friend

CONTENTS

Chapter		Page
1	IN THE BEGINNING	17
2	WHAT A PANIC!	25
3	DREAM HOME	31
4	THE 'C' WORD!	39
5	AN ANGEL CALLED BOB	45
6	LETTING GOD IN	57
7	THE POWER OF PRAYER	63
8	BLESSINGS IN DISGUISE	71
9	STOP, LOOK AND LISTEN!	79
10	PLUGGED IN!	87
11	THE BIG PICTURE	93
12	BODY AND SOUL	99
13	A TRUE BELIEVER	105
14	MY HEAVENLY FATHER	115
15	HOW CANCER SAVED MY LIFE	121
16	AN UPDATE	125
17	IN CLOSING	129

Amazing grace!
How sweet the sound
That saved a wretch
Like me
I once was lost,
But now am found,
Was blind, but now I see.

                        John Newton

Prelude . . .

I would like to share with you some of my personal journey, my spiritual quest. I hope that, in some special way it may help you to find what you may have lost, or what you may desperately be seeking. It may awaken your own spirituality or help to restore and rejuvenate your own faith. It may provide you with more insight, make things clearer for you or at least offer some food for thought. Better yet, it may eliminate fears and anxieties, which will help to guide you toward a life filled with contentment and joy and offer hope for the future.

Between the pages of this book lie my own personal thoughts and feelings. You may beg to differ and I respect your right to your own beliefs and values. It is not my intention to force my faith upon you, simply to share a part of my own exciting journey.

Discovering God, or re-discovering Him, has been a life-altering event. It is something wonderful that has happened to me: An experience of a lifetime.

Mary Jane Warr

God's Perfect Knowledge of Man

For You formed my inward parts; you covered me in my mother's womb.
I will praise You,
for I am fearfully and wonderfully made.
Marvelous are Your works,
and that my soul knows very well.

My frame was not hidden from You, when I was made in secret,
and skillfully wrought in the lowest parts of the earth.

Your eyes saw my substance, being yet unformed.
And in Your book they all were written,
the days fashioned for me, when as yet there were none of them.

How precious also are Your thoughts to me, O God!
How great is the sum of them!
If I should count them,
they would be more in number than the sand:
when I awake, I am still with You.

Psalm 139: 13 – 18

Mary Jane Warr

Mary Jane Warr

1
IN THE BEGINNING

All happy families resemble one another: every unhappy family is unhappy in its own way.
Tolstoy

I was born and raised in England during World War II. My father was in the Royal Air Force and he was stationed somewhere far away. By the time I was nine my parent's marriage had disintegrated. They went their separate ways and later divorced. My family consisted of my mother, my brother David who was eighteen months older than I, and myself.

We visited my grandparents frequently. They lived in a wonderful seaside town, whereas we lived in a bedroom community near London, close to the air raids. When Mum moved in with the new man in her life, my brother chose to stay with her. But something inside of me, my intuition, told me to go with my grandparents, even though it was very hard to leave Mum and David behind. While I was always somewhat fearful of my grandfather, it turned out that, in spite of my tender years, I had made the right decision and my grandparents became my surrogate parents from then on.

When I think about it, I believe that the only thing my parents actually had in common was their religious background. My maternal grandparents were dedicated Congregationalists, and my paternal grandparents were devoted Wesleyans. My paternal grandfather was a missionary who travelled many times to Canada, preaching the religious teachings of John Wesley who founded the Wesleyan Church back in the 18th century. I don't remember my paternal grandparents at all.

While my mother did not go to church herself, she always made sure that David and I attended

Sunday school. When I became a ward of my grandparents it was church and Sunday school on Sunday mornings, bible study group on Sunday afternoon, and church again most Sunday evenings. While in church, I remember my mind would wander because the readings seemed long and boring and I didn't understand the words. I did poorly in the bible study group as I just couldn't concentrate and would daydream. Things were going over my head. I loved to sing the hymns, though.

I had the same problem in school. As an adult, I now realize that I was probably suffering from childhood depression, which was not recognized in those days. I was full of confusion and anxieties, perhaps due to the worry, stress and sadness of my family situation. I missed my parents and my brother so much and had no contact with any of them. While living with my grandparents I was obviously in the midst of an environment that believed in prayer and in God as a male entity. Grace was said before every meal and prayers were always said on bended knee at bedtime. I would pray for the usual kid things such as a puppy or a pony. I prayed that my parents would get back together and I wanted David to be with me, but these things didn't happen. I don't remember questioning God about my unanswered prayers. Praying was something I did automatic-ally before bedtime. I discovered that it was a good way of delaying the inevitable "good nights" by a few more minutes! God's name seemed to be everywhere in my life. It was just a household word. At school we sang hymns and said prayers at morning assembly because religious education was just a regular part of the school curriculum.

When I was about eleven years old, I remember praying really hard. I wanted so much to attend private girls' school rather than a regular school. I was a shy child and didn't look forward to attending the senior school, which was much bigger than the school I had attended. I had two cousins who attended a convent school and I was envious of them. They talked about their small classes and the individual attention they received. I loved the look of their smart uniforms. I always felt they were much better and more deserving than I was. I would pray really, really hard each night. But nothing happened. Eventually, I plucked up some courage and wrote to my father, who was financially responsible for me and pleaded with him to allow me to go to a private school. The reply was a definite, "NO!" That was the first time I remember asking my father for anything and the first time that I felt angry with God. It seemed as though He had really let me down. I did not want to go to the local senior school. I felt disappointed and hopeless.

I disliked school and felt very unhappy almost every day for the rest of my school years. My saving grace was my best friend, Diane. I was so very glad that we met, as we became constant companions. Somehow we got through school together. Like the kindred spirits that we were, we still keep in touch with one another more than fifty years later.

By the time I was fourteen my grand- mother was seriously ill with terminal colon cancer. I remember praying and praying to God for her to be spared, that He would let her live. My prayers became obsessive and I tried to emphasize them with a system of counting. Each alternate stair became a "yes" or a "no." "Yes", she would die or "No", she would not. Of course I always made it work out that the answer was "No", she would not die. Naively, I never thought that my Gran would actually die. But God had other plans and Gran was set free from this earth and her pain and suffering. I watched innocently as she went through her pain and torment and her eventual death. In fact, I was the last person she spoke to before she died. I was left with a big hole in my heart and utter despondency. Once again, I was angry with God.

He had taken my Gran, my lifeline, from me. I felt very much alone.

My grandfather was an authoritative and autocratic man with a bad temper that could flare up at any time. He was unpredictable, so it was difficult to trust him, even though there was a good sense of humour lurking behind the stern demeanor.

As I got older I began to see him more and more for the hypocrite that he was. He was a leading figure in our community, well respected for his good deeds and recognized as a devout and regular churchgoer. But at home, away from the eyes of those who looked up to him, this pillar of rectitude was very different. For several years this paragon of virtue was actually engaged in a pattern of regular sexual abuse of me, his granddaughter! I survived this abuse but I have found it difficult to forgive him. I still see his hypocrisy as extreme and very irreverent.

After Gran's death, my grandfather had to find a live-in housekeeper to look after us. Gwen was chosen from the many applicants. She was a personable, neat and tidy woman with a cute little daughter. Gwen was considerably younger than my grandfather was. Once she and her daughter moved in to our house life really began to change. Granddad soon became enamored with Gwen, and they married within months of Gran's passing.

I felt betrayed. In my confusion and anger I started telephoning my father, who by this time was also remarried. Somehow he knew that Gran had passed away. I asked him if I could come and live with him. Dad seemed pleased at my request and soon arrangements were made for me to go and live with him and his new wife.

Dad was still the devout man that I remembered him to be. But I soon saw him as weak and ineffective, lacking any kind of backbone. His new wife was a very stern and domineering woman, autocratic and very controlling. Like Granddad, she had a bad temper and was unpredictable. I was afraid of her wrath so I soon learned to toe the line. My father was vulnerable and quite unable to protect himself. My stepmother could easily overpower him. He couldn't defend himself so he certainly couldn't stand up for me. He was emotionally unavailable. I never felt that I trusted him to be there for me, to protect me. I felt alone again. There was no one in my life to comfort me or to make me feel secure.

My stepmother possessed a great sense of humor under her bristling veneer, which only made the situation more confusing. She was not a churchgoer herself and she was highly critical of Dad's need to attend church, calling him a fraud and other names. I felt like a thorn in her side, but I couldn't blame her for that. In a way, I had been forced into her life. Living with my stepmother in control meant no more church or grace at mealtimes, unless you wished to be verbally abused or ridiculed. Bedtime was strictly for sleeping, no more prayers on bended knee, goodnight kisses or affection. It was an entirely different way of living. I would say prayers quietly to myself once in a while, mostly for my own comfort, I think.

In 1954, when I was sixteen, my father, stepmother and I emigrated to Canada and settled in the Toronto area. Prior to our emigration I was briefly reunited with Mum and David. Dad encouraged David to emigrate also and he went to Canada ahead of us. It felt good to be with my family although I knew that things would never be the same again. The original dynamics of my family had changed irreversibly, but I looked forward to starting a new life in a new land.

Mary Jane Warr

2
WHAT A PANIC!

We are healed of a suffering only by experiencing it in full.
Marcel Proust

By the time I was eleven years old, I had developed agoraphobia. I found myself afraid of almost everything: going to school, going to church, going to movies, theatres and stores. Even normally pleasant occasions would be spoilt for me by persistent and extreme bouts of high anxiety. I suffered terribly from panic attacks, which seemed to appear at the slightest provocation and afterwards I would start to anticipate the next one, which kept me in a never-ending state of fear. Probably this was the result of all the insecurities caused by my dysfunctional upbringing. Even at school it was difficult to carry on a "normal", carefree life because the panic disorder was always there and in the way. No one seemed to understand why I acted "strangely" at times. I didn't understand it myself and couldn't explain to anyone what I was feeling and experiencing. If I had tried to explain, I doubt that anyone would have listened or understood. I thought I had done a good job of hiding my fears and tried to appear as "normal" as the next person even if inwardly I was petrified, filled with panic and anxiety. I was certainly afraid of my fear, which at that time had no name. I didn't have a clue about life or how to cope with things, especially the things that frightened me.

As I approached my twenties, my unpredictable panic attacks were becoming increasingly worse. I was experiencing an attack several times each day, but I managed to work for a large company in Toronto. I commuted to work more than an hour each way from the suburbs. At times the daily panic grind became unbearable. Finally, I was forced to get down on my knees each morning before I left home for the office and pray hard, "Please God, take away these frightening feelings. Let me get through this day without experiencing them. Just one day." This went on for months and months but the panic did not dissipate. In fact, the attacks seemed to grow stronger than ever.

I was still living in an unhealthy environment. Dad and his wife seemed unhappy most of the time. I never felt safe, secure or protected as I was still surrounded by neurotic people. No wonder I had phobias! I had the opportunity to move out and live with friends but I was too insecure to leave home. Just about everything I did was motivated by fear.

One day, I felt so disgusted that I said, childishly, "Okay God, that is it. I'm never going to ask you for another thing. I asked to go to private school and you ignored me. You've taken away my mother, my brother and my Gran. Now you won't stop these frightening feelings. I no longer believe in you." I remember deliberately turning my back on God. I was in a huff and having a temper tantrum. I felt jubilant but also very guilty. That was the day I closed my heart. I decided that I was an agnostic. I also became a cynic.

Life went on. The sky didn't fall and I wasn't struck by lightning. In fact, I met a very nice young man by the name of Ernie. He was a friend of my brother David, who introduced us within a few days of our arriving in Canada. Like us, Ernie had emigrated from England with his family, only five years earlier, so we had much in common. We dated, on and off, for several years before becoming serious about each other. We married when I was twenty-four years old. Ernie turned my life around for the better. He was, and still is, my knight in shining armor, my Rock of Gibraltar. He is, by far, the kindest person that I know. He is non-judgmental, loving and extremely patient, he understands me and I trust him implicitly. He showed me what unconditional love is. He has always loved me for who I am. He helped me to receive the very best care that I needed for my panic disorder and emotional confusion. I was fortunate to have the finest specialist that Toronto had to offer at that time. It was a long and painful journey but Ernie was at my side the whole time. He has always supported me in whatever I have wanted to do. I wouldn't trade him for the world. Ernie has been, and still is, an excellent father to our son Jeff and an equally wonderful grandfather to our granddaughters. What a blessing he is!

We survived the usual teen-years conflicts with Jeff and we all came through the other side with a few battle scars, but our little family has remained very much intact. The panic disorder is now a thing of the past, thank goodness. I worked through my fear of intimacy and rejection with my family, but I continued to keep God separate and at arm's length.

Ernie was in the banking business and was required to relocate from time to time. His big promotion came in 1979 and he was transferred to Calgary, Alberta. It was difficult leaving Toronto. We had good friends there but it was time to move. Ernie enjoyed the more laid-back environment that Calgary offered and the challenge of his new position. I decided to take the bull by the horns and start my own business as a counselor and therapist. Despite having had no formal training in the field, I had plenty of personal experience to draw from. I was very lucky that the specialist who treated me in Toronto had seen my potential to become a therapist. At the end of my treatment, he took me under his wing and I worked in his office as his personal secretary for a few years. He included me in his therapy groups and workshops. As a special guest he invited me to attend conferences and conventions centered about fears, phobias and anxieties. Through him I was introduced to some very prominent people in the field of behavior therapy, psychiatry and psychology. It's as though I was in the right place at the right time. I received excellent training because of that good doctor's faith in me.

In Calgary, my private practice flourished and life was good. But in spite of that, I had a deep feeling of restlessness and personal dissatisfaction. I tried to figure it out, but couldn't understand why. I even tried more therapy, after which I thought I really did know myself inside out. I worked even harder to try and satisfy my uneasiness. At times I felt guilty for these discontented feelings because, generally speaking, life was good and I was more than grateful for that. We were able to travel quite a bit and lived a comfortable and happy life, or so I thought.

Then, one snowy night in January, Ernie took the dog for her usual evening walk. Unfortunately, (or was it?), he slipped on a patch of ice and was badly injured. For the next four months he was flat on his back in the hospital, his shattered femur held together with an orthopedic pin and stretched in traction. He was truly confined to barracks. He obviously needed a long break!

This accident, and his long recovery time, gave Ernie plenty of time to think. As a result he finally admitted to himself, and then to me, that he was discontented with his professional life. He had enjoyed a successful career, but banking as he knew it was changing and he didn't particularly like the look of the future. He had become disillusioned and felt that the banking business was no longer for him.

I could see that he was depressed at the thought of returning to work. It was at this time that we began to think about taking an early retirement. The bank was in a state of flux and the future was uncertain. Why not throw in the towel now and take our chances? It took a year or so to make all the necessary arrangements for his departure but it was one of the very best things he has ever done. Ernie has no regrets and he has never looked back.

Mary Jane Warr

3
DREAM HOME

Pride goes before destruction, and a haughty spirit before a fall.
                    Proverbs 16: 18

In our many travels, we had always kept our eyes open for a Shangri La for our retirement. After much searching we decided upon the West Coast, particularly Vancouver Island. The lush terrain, the Pacific Ocean, temperate climate and soft air, appealed to us. We had been city suburban folk for most of our lives, and we were both ready for a change of pace and scenery and for the benefits of country living. This seemed like the perfect spot.

In June of 1990, I closed my practice. Ernie had been retired for a couple of years and was waiting for me to slow down and eventually retire. The time was right. We had already purchased a one-acre property on Vancouver Island, in a quiet rural setting some time before we were ready to build our "dream home." We had all of our plans and blueprints in place. Jeff was coming with us to help us build. Also, a friend of ours who had been a builder at one time was moving out to the coast at the same time as us. He offered to help us build the house by being our contractor.

Despite all our plans, our dream home soon turned into a living nightmare. It felt as though God was up to His tricks again. Nothing went right. Our plans disintegrated before our eyes, everything that could go wrong did go wrong. Things were completely out of control. The end result was that we not only lost our dream home but most of our retirement fund along with it. We were forced to sell our home before it was finished. We had no one to blame but our naive and inexperienced selves. We felt as though we would never recover financially from this loss.

In our state of grief, shock and depression we purchased another home, this time in a city subdivision. We lived there eleven months! One day Ernie said, "We did not come to the coast to live in the city. We came here to live in the country and that's where we should be." He was right, so we set about finding an affordable country home. At one time we had seriously considered building a home on Gabriola Island, and now it seemed to beckon us once again.

Gabriola is one of the many Gulf Islands located in the Strait of Georgia, off the western mainland. Gabriola is a jewel, about 14 kilometers long by 4.5 kilometers wide with a coastline of about 45 kilometers and a population of about 4,000 people. Gabriola has lots of amenities for an island of its size.

Gabriolans get the best of laidback living but with most of the services they require. The City of Nanaimo is a twenty minute ferry ride away And Vancouver, with all the conveniences of a large city, is just a few minutes away by floatplane, or a couple of hours by ferry.

Fortunately, we found a little country home that exactly suited our needs. At this point it looked very good to us. A small three-bedroom bungalow on an attractive half-acre wooded lot seemed heavenly after all we had been through. Our priorities had really changed – for the better. It was as though this move was meant to happen. Everything went right and fell into place. Our suburban home in Nanaimo sold quickly with an early possession date and our country home was brand new and vacant. We could move in whenever we chose.

The move itself was interesting. We were downsizing from a two-storey, 2,500 square foot house with plenty of storage and cupboard space, to a bungalow less than half that size, with very limited storage. We took advantage of the situation and did what we had often dreamed of doing by completely changing our lifestyle to a less materialistic one with a much slower pace. We started by going through all of our personal effects and letting go of all the "city" stuff, from clothing to furniture. We had to be ruthless. It was hard to let go of some of the lovely things we had collected over the years, but they were just "things." They were not making us happy and we no longer needed them. We had a bumper garage sale, which produced some revenue. It was goodbye to competitive and somewhat formal urban/suburban living.

We moved into our country home and we named it Grove Cottage, because it sits amid a grove of tall trees. We were down to the bare essentials and started reconstructing our lives and decorating our new home. We visited country specialty stores looking for pine furniture. We found many pieces we liked, but our hearts dropped when we looked at price tags. There was no way we could afford to buy this kind of furniture. It was back to the drawing board once more.

Ernie had always been interested in woodwork and he had taken a good look at the construction of the various pieces. One day he said, "You know, if I put my mind to it I think I could build a Welsh dresser. At least I'm willing to try. What do you think?" He took me by surprise. "Do you really think you could?" I replied, trying not to be the least bit doubtful. After an excited discussion, Ernie agreed to try his hand at making a Welsh dresser, an informal buffet and china cabinet combined, to his own design.

He has always enjoyed working with wood. As a boy, he had proudly earned his Boy Scout carpenter's badge as well as a first prize certificate at a Scoutcraft exhibition. At home he made various items on his own for special family presents. Both of his grandfathers were master carpenters so he came by his talent and love of woodwork quite naturally. He admitted that he had never taken on a project of that size before.

First of all, he and our son Jeff had great fun building a small workshop on our property. Ernie designed it himself and made everything, even the windows. It was small, but now he had a place of his very own in which to work. A dream came true for him.

The Welsh dresser was wonderful. It wasn't factory-perfect, but it was perfect in its own way. Today, it is much admired by visitors. Not only is it a very functional piece of furniture but it is also an heirloom for our family. It remains my favorite piece. Ernie really found his niche and has made us more and more lovely matching pieces. It is rewarding to see him so relaxed and happy. He deserves to feel content.

On Saturday mornings throughout the summer season there is a Farmer's Market here on Gabriola. It is a meeting place for many island artisans and provides an opportunity for them to sell their wares. Ernie loves to attend as a vendor, a far cry from the city bank manager! Not only does it provide a small source of income for us, but most of all it gives him so much pleasure. Gabriola has given Ernie the opportunity to be himself. It has provided him with a new level of confidence and personal satisfaction. His creativity, hidden away and left dormant for so many years, has emerged and has an outlet.

Due to our financial situation I reluctantly agreed to go back to work and start a new practice in Nanaimo. So much for my retirement! I placed an ad in the local newspaper and presto, people responded. I kept my practice small, as I only wanted to work part time. The ferry commute proved to be relaxing and a good way to get to know some of the other islanders. My practice went well. I met some very nice people and made some good friends along the way. In the end I was glad that I went back to work. I retired again in December 2000, after a total of twenty-five enjoyable years as a personal counselor and therapist.

Gabriola turned out to be a little piece of paradise. It is truly beautiful. Not only does it have beaches and tidal pools but also many trees, birds and wildlife. It is a friendly, yet quiet, community. There are many talented, gentle folk who have chosen to live here.

Gabriola has provided us with a wonderful sense of belonging, which is truly a gift in itself. Each day I enjoy a long walk with Brandy, our Airedale Terrier. At first we would go exploring, as the territory was new to both of us. Unfortunately, Ernie could not join us on our walks because of a degenerative disease that is attacking his spine, making long walks difficult for him. I did my best to fill him in when we returned home each day.

On one of our walks I discovered a beautiful spot which had a magnificent view of the Strait of Georgia. One could see the northeastern coastline of Vancouver Island on the left and the northwestern coastline of the mainland on the right hand side, complete with snow-capped mountains that swept down to the sparkling sea. I told myself that this must be a piece of heaven. It is the kind of view that is simply astounding. The view was visible amid a curtain of tall trees. It was so peaceful and quiet, not another living soul around; just the soaring eagles, Brandy and me. This spot felt like mine and I claimed it that day as my "special place." A place to be contemplative.

I visited my special place frequently and always experienced the same feelings of awe and tranquility. Some days it would produce strong, almost overwhelming feelings of joy, delight and gratitude in my heart. What a wonderful place to call home. I began to question how and why we were so lucky to be living in such a beautiful part of the world. I would think about our grueling journey that seemed to lead us here.

At times I, "Mary the Cynic", would allow my thoughts to go deeper to a more philosophical or spiritual place, where I began to think about how all of this beauty came to be. I started thinking more about God but I used the name "Creator", as I still felt the need to keep a little distance between the two of us. I had to admit He was something of a phenomenon and I would ask, "Who are you?" and "What do you do?" and "How do you do it?"

I came to the conclusion that He is an unexplainable force who has created all things. That there are some things we just aren't supposed to know or understand but that there is a reason for everything, including the things that happen to us all. We may think that we control our lives, but do we really?

I had many conversations with the Creator. Mostly they would relate to the beauty of the island but sometimes I would share my worries and concerns with Him. If I were looking for answers to problems I would ask the Creator to show me the way. It was comforting. I noticed myself looking for answers but not really expecting any replies. One day, at my special place, I observed that there are two sets of mountains, one on each side of the vista, and I found myself reciting a piece from the bible, Psalm 121, "I will lift up my eyes unto the hills -- from where will my help come? My help comes from the Lord, who made heaven and earth." It was magically impacting. I also surprised myself that I had actually remembered this passage from Sunday bible studies many years before.

From that point on, whenever I had a problem I would go to my special place and recite this piece. I guess I was really beginning to look for some answers, perhaps with God in mind. Was there a change in attitude occurring here? Why were we now living in this perfect environment? Could it be that this is what God had intended for us all along? That He was trying to steer us clear of the "perfect" dream home and we just weren't listening to His warning? I then began to see clearly that our dream home would have been a big burden in so many ways. It would have been a huge property for us to look after, not a sensible plan for Ernie, with his back condition. As it was situated in quite a prestigious area we would still be in the trap of keeping up with the neighbors, something we both wanted to get away from. Maybe all of our heartache was for a reason, including the loss of our money. Was it Providence? God's way of protecting us?

Grove Cottage on Gabriola Island has more than proved to be our dream home. It is where we belong and we love it dearly.

Mary Jane Warr

4

THE 'C' WORD!

The man who fears suffering is already suffering from what he fears.

Michel De Montaigne

I always had the feeling that one day I would have to face cancer. It was a gut instinct, a hunch, my sixth sense working overtime or perhaps a foregone conclusion due to my family history. The thought of cancer and accompanying chemotherapy terrified me, in fact became a real dread. There is one school of thought that believes that if you dread an illness enough you can actually produce it. The mind is a powerful tool.

Of course, the inevitable happened. In September 1995, a mass was discovered in my breast during a routine mammogram and a biopsy was ordered. The prospects were very frightening, to say the least. I was so afraid that I visited my special spot and actually talked to God. Game over! I needed to talk to the "Big Guy in the Sky" himself. I told him how sorry I was that I had played the role of the cynic and turned my back on Him, but if ever I needed Him, it was now. I prayed so hard for His forgiveness and found myself bargaining with Him if He would spare me. I wasn't anywhere near ready to leave this good earth, especially as we had discovered Gabriola and the sweet life. I lifted up my eyes to those hills and asked for His help. My prayers were urgent, sincere and said with conviction. I asked that He be with me all the way and to somehow show me a sign, or a signal, that He was with me.

My surgeon arranged to do the biopsy in the emergency department of the hospital, as the surgery itself was a small, localized procedure. He said that he had chosen a time when it would be quiet in the emergency department. I must admit that I am not at all happy in a hospital setting, remnants of the past, I guess. Give me the dentist any day!

So, not only was I petrified of the unknown, the procedure itself and its outcome, but I was fearful of going into the emergency department. I was in a terrible dither that day and kept praying to God for His assistance.

My heart was beating overtime when I arrived at the hospital. Greeted by friendly staff, I was ushered through the emergency department into a curtained area. My surgeon was paged and I was told to put on a gown, relax and lie on the gurney and wait for him to arrive. As I lay there I noticed how peaceful and quiet it was. There wasn't a person within hearing distance. The doctor was right, he had picked a quiet time. I checked in with God to see if He was around. As I did so a cool breeze came from nowhere. It brushed the curtains around me and they moved gently. The light wind touched my face as it passed through. I immediately felt, and knew, that God was with me. I was convinced He was watching over me and I was calm. He had answered my prayers. I remember reading a little piece in a magazine which said, "Often we want to hear God speak with clarity of thunder and storm, yet God speaks loudest in a whisper." Sometimes we need to be astute when listening or looking for God.

When the surgeon arrived, he couldn't have been kinder. While he performed the biopsy, he put me at ease by chatting about everyday things. The procedure was over before I knew it. The end result was fine.

After the lump was analyzed the pathologist agreed it was just fatty tissue. Panic over. I went to my special spot and gave thanks to God. I was now very humble before Him. There was no doubt in my mind that He had been with me all the way.

Then, in November 1997, to my horror, I discovered another lump in my breast in the same vicinity during a breast self-examination. I tried not to panic this time and told myself that in all probability it was just more fatty tissue, promising that if it were still there in December, I would see the doctor. You guessed it, yes it was still there. Meanwhile, I had stepped up the prayers considerably, mostly asking God to be with me, and please, no cancer.

I made an appointment with my family physician who arranged a mammogram at the hospital for me. The initial result from the mammogram was that it was scar tissue from my previous biopsy. But fortunately I was referred to my surgeon once more. He was very prudent and carefully assessed the situation recommending that another biopsy be done, just to be sure. He took five samples of tissue during this procedure and when the pathologist's report came back it stated that 3 millimeters of cancer cells had been discovered. I was given the news at my next appointment. What a shock and what a wakeup call! It was as though the blood in my veins had turned to ice water. Everything seemed surreal. My dread had become a reality. I felt as though God had let me down again.

My surgeon reassured me that my cancer was in early stages and it was the slow growth kind. He admitted that he didn't know how much cancer remained in my body as he had sliced through the tumor during the biopsy.

A lumpectomy was scheduled within two weeks. No time was wasted. This time it was real surgery, full anesthetic and a night in the hospital. The surgeon said he would not only remove the mass but the auxiliary lymph nodes as well, just to make sure. I sank into a depression. How could God do this to me?

At my follow-up appointment the surgeon assured me that he had removed all of the remaining cancer cells, and that the lymph nodes were clear. The pathologist's report verified this. Good news. What a relief! As far as he was concerned my cancer was gone. Because of the size of the tumor, although small, the surgeon felt I should go to the cancer clinic in Vancouver for an assessment, as there were no facilities in Nanaimo at that time. It was arranged for me to see one of the top breast cancer specialists in British Columbia. Was there a God after all? This meant that I had to go to yet another hospital setting. I can tell you, in all honesty, that I didn't look forward to a large facility that specialized in cancer! Two dreads rolled up into one. I realized that Vancouver's cancer clinic was going to be a large city hospital and that I'd better get used to the idea of going there. My visit had to be if I wanted to see this thing through and to be truly cancer free. My stress level reached an all-time high. I had no option but to call on God for His help. So I lifted up my eyes once again and called out for HELP!

The A. Maxwell Evans Clinic in Vancouver was a huge six-storey facility that spread over a city block. My suspicions were confirmed. Ernie, my faithful companion, was at my side. Inside the cancer clinic there were very few windows but it was bright and cheerfully decorated. It was a bustling, busy place. People, people everywhere. Some looked very ill and pale as they lay on their hospital beds, or were propped up in wheelchairs hooked up to intravenous equipment with tubes extending from their poor bodies.

Then there were the lucky ones like me who appeared to be hale and hearty. The corridors were long and narrow with other corridors shooting off in all directions to waiting rooms, therapy rooms and so on. It was like a rabbit warren – a claustrophobic's nightmare.

The breast cancer specialist was wonderful. After the assessment he recommended a course of radiation therapy as a precautionary measure. The radiation would knock out any stray cells that may be lurking, reducing the chances of a reoccurrence from 30 per cent to 10 per cent. I was certainly in favor of preventative measures, especially at this stage of the game. I was so grateful that there would be no chemotherapy, that the thought of the actual radiation didn't seem bad at all. Thank you God!

It was agreed that I should be placed on the waiting list for nineteen sessions of radiation therapy at the Vancouver cancer clinic. The wait seemed endless. But several weeks later "the call" came, allowing me 24 hours' notice to inform my clients, who were aware of my situation, and were prepared to wait for my return. Bless their hearts. I also had to get myself psyched up to live "somewhere" in Vancouver for a month.

Mary Jane Warr

5
AN ANGEL CALLED BOB

Angel (n):

an attendant or messenger of God; a spiritual being employed in the service of God; a person with qualities of such a spirit, as gentleness, purity, etc.; person who resembles an angel in attributes or actions.

The cancer clinic arranged accommodation for my stay in Vancouver. I was to stay at Vancouver Lodge, a well-equipped residence for out-of-town people who are receiving cancer treatment. Meals would be provided, for a minimal cost, in a bright dining room and there were 34 bedrooms on a shared accommodation basis, no private rooms. The Lodge, which is owned and operated by The Canadian Cancer Society, is across the street from the A. Maxwell Evans Clinic so it was handy for daily treatments and for doctor's appointments. I was able to commute home at the weekends. Thank you, God!

Before I left for Vancouver, I told Ernie that while I was at the cancer clinic I would try to arrange a meeting with the chaplain. I felt the need to do some serious talking about God and spirituality. Ernie, in his inimitable style, showed no sign of surprise at what I thought was an outrageous statement. In fact, as usual, he was most supportive. After thinking about it I guessed he really wasn't too surprised as I share everything with him. He knew about my special spot and my talks with my Creator/God. He said that if it would help me then he didn't have a problem with it. I promised that I was not planning to become a religious fanatic!

I arrived at The Lodge midafternoon Wednesday, April 1st (no fooling!). I stood alone in the middle of a big strange city wondering what I was about to face. My first session was booked for early Thursday morning. Ernie dropped me off at the front door of The Lodge and I had time to recover from saying goodbye to him and to acquaint myself with my new roommate and surroundings.

I must admit I was concerned, not only about the treatment, but also the shared accommodation. I need not have worried. Lucy, my new roommate was a sweet and bright lady of 79 years. She had arrived a couple of days ahead of me and had already had two overnight "roomies" before me. She was pleased to hear that I was going to stay for a while. We took to one another straight away and had fun in our own way. We could easily make one another laugh, even on those down days. Lucy was a devout Jehovah's Witness. She would earnestly read her scriptures, which she said brought her great comfort, and I truly believe they did. I found it calming to have a roommate who was gentle, loving and kind. A believer in her faith, Lucy was a good role model.

I explored The Lodge from top to bottom. When I took the elevator up to the dining room I noticed a sign posted on the elevator wall announcing a weekly spiritual group discussion which was to be held in the conference room, at 7 p.m. that evening. The sign read: "Nondenominational. Everyone welcome." I suddenly felt empowered and decided to attend, putting my fears aside. After all, I had nothing else to do and I thought it might be a good way to meet some other residents. I was about to embark on my quest.

Nervously, at 7 p.m., I entered the conference room, which was situated at the end of a long hallway. The door was wide open and there were sounds of voices and laughter echoing down the hallway. As I entered, I saw half a dozen or so men and women, casually seated in a circle. Bob, the group leader, welcomed me in a sincere and friendly way. He made me feel right at home and accepted. After a few minutes of polite waiting for late comers, Bob started the evening by welcoming the new members to the group and introducing himself. He was a fourth year divinity student at Regent College in Vancouver. This was his final year of studies and he chose to work at the cancer clinic in Vancouver for his practicum. Besides assisting the chaplain at the clinic, he volunteered to run the Lodge group. His overseer was a mature woman from a Baptist church. She was his mentor and allowed him to run the group with free reins. Bob was nearing the end of his final year. There was something special about him, and I felt sure he was put in my life for a reason.

Bob worked his way around the group asking each person to give their name. If they wanted to add more information they were free to do so. I was convinced that I was the only new person there. Wrong! Half the group were new like me but you'd never know it because they were all so friendly and at ease with one another. I guess having cancer as a common denominator has its advantages. We were all handed packages of interesting reading material and pertinent information. This was our initiation.

The first woman Bob addressed gave her name willingly. I think it was Brenda. She told us that this was to be her last night at the group, she was not a new member. She went on to say that she had been released from the cancer clinic and was about to go home. Those who knew Brenda from the previous weeks seemed genuinely sorry to see her go. They all wished her well and asked her how she felt about leaving the clinic. Brenda said that she was ready to go. I thought how lucky she was to be going home. I found out that she had braved chemotherapy, radiation and surgery.

I thought her to be wonderfully brave as she had gone through all of those scary treatments and come out the other side. She was now completely finished and deserved to go home.

Bob moved on to the next person, and the next, each of them volunteering their names and information about themselves and their cancer. When it came to my turn I could feel my heart pound. I hadn't spoken to many people about my breast cancer and I wasn't sure I was too keen on the idea even now. I wasn't ashamed of the disease, I guess I'm just a private person. But I found myself giving my name clearly, telling them where I lived and revealing to the group the source of my cancer. As I spoke those few words I noticed a few women in the circle nodding their heads, they were kindred spirits. I began to relax and enjoy this new experience.

After Bob had done a sweep of the group he came back and asked each person if they had any concerns they would like to share. Brenda emphatically said "No", she had no concerns and she was ready to go. Bob nodded and said that he understood and proceeded to the next person. Each of us had concerns. Mine was that I was to start my treatment the next day in the dreaded cancer clinic and I didn't know what to expect, so naturally I was concerned. That was an understatement! Bob noted each person's worry and anxiety with interest. He was an excellent listener. When he finished going around the group he proceeded to say a personalized prayer for each and every one of us. I found this to be a wonderful experience. Many years ago when I attended church it seemed to me that the minister or pastor always read impersonal prayers from a book. Bob's eloquent prayer, straight from the heart, was just for me. He used my name and asked God to watch over me and to bless me as I headed to the clinic for my first session. This prayer did wonders for my spirits. They were really lifted. I was flying high and felt a surge of hopefulness. I felt like a woman with a mission. My quest had begun.

In the discussion that evening, Bob talked about God, The Good Shepherd, rescuing lost sheep and lambs. When He found one He would lift the little one up and hold it warmly and lovingly in His arms. Bob suggested that those of us who felt lost see themselves as one of those lambs. God would be delighted to save us from harm and danger, as He loved us because we were His own, now and forever. We needed to realize that God loves to take people who appear to be lost and turn them around. Another way of looking at it is that when we slip off of the rails God puts us back on the right track and may head us off in a different direction. He wants to make the rest of our life the best of our life. This analogy was not new but I guess I wasn't really open to it before. It was food for thought. I must admit that it was hard to believe that God did really love me.

I joined in the open discussion and found it stimulating to be with like-minded people.

It was about now that Bob said they always sang a hymn together. As I pulled the hymn sheet from my package the hymn looked unfamiliar to me. It was called, "Safe in the Shadow of the Lord." Once we started to sing I felt a little silly singing out loud in such a small group but I really enjoyed the words and the tune. It was touching.

> *Safe in the shadow of the Lord*
> *Beneath His hand and power*
> *I trust in Him, I trust in Him,*
> *My fortress and my tower.*

As the hymn progressed I began to feel very emotional and I was amazed at the tears welling up inside me. I told myself that it was a tension release, which may have been true, but I felt it was far more than that. I felt God's presence in that room just as I had in the emergency department when I had my biopsy done. He was really there for me and touching my heart.

As the evening came to a close Bob said a final goodbye prayer for Brenda, which was so nice. We were invited to stay for tea or coffee and a selection of home-made goodies, courtesy of Bob, who baked them himself! The evening ended on an up note. All those who knew Brenda gave her big goodbye hugs and kisses, which brought tears to her eyes. But there was much laughter and lightness.

I don't think I have ever been in the company of people like this before. We bonded so quickly. I guess we were all desperately hanging on by our finger nails, seeking cures, solace, comfort, answers, hope and maybe if we were really lucky, some of us lost souls might even find God, in our hour of need.

I found that just being in The Lodge opened my eyes; it was an educational experience. There were patients of all ages, from all walks of life and from all over British Columbia and the Yukon Territories, with an assortment of cancers. There was a husband and wife there, both receiving treatment for their respective cancers. We were all at various stages of our disease and treatment. It was a very humbling experience. I was most amazed at the smokers among them. They would assemble in an outdoor designated smoking area to have a puff on their cigarettes, regardless of the fact that many were hooked up to monitors, while others would gasp for air and cough profusely. I questioned whether they really did want to beat their cancer.

The next morning I had to get up early for my appointment with the specialist. I was nervous as I prepared for my first solo to the clinic. Ernie had been with me for my assessment several weeks before, but now I was starting "my journey" alone. I knew that Ernie was still behind me emotionally but I also knew that this was something I had to do by myself. The thought of going to the clinic terrified me but I had to go, there was no way around it. So I swallowed hard and entered the building. I felt weak from fear. There was no one to hold onto but myself. What a pathetic mess! Suddenly I remembered Bob's prayer. "Dear God. Please watch over Mary as she heads to the clinic tomorrow. Please relieve her of her concerns and bless her." Pow! I calmed right down. My knees became strong. I was fine and my mind was clear.

In fact, the appointment went very well. It was sort of an initiation appointment, complete with a video about radiation, a tour of the facilities including the radiation department, which was down one of those rabbit warrens! The radiation room was quite large, with no windows of course, and a low ceiling. The room was obviously well insulated because of the high levels of radiation. The machine sat alone in the center of the room; I was first given a small tattoo mark on my breast and then shown how the technicians would "sculpt" my body into the correct position for the therapy, using this mark to set the machine into the precise position required. They moved the machine around a bit so that I could get used to the noises that would occur with each movement. Soft music was playing and the air was pleasantly cool and well circulated. No feelings of claustrophobia here! The procedure itself didn't sound too threatening and was scheduled to begin the next day. I floated out of the building on a cushion of air. My heart was light. I guess Bob's prayer really worked and God was listening to him. I couldn't wait for the following Wednesday night to arrive so that I could tell everyone about my positive adventure.

The following day was the first radiation therapy. Even though everything had been explained to me the previous day my mind seemed to leave my body at the front door of the building! The apprehension of what was about to happen became greater than anything else. Somehow I managed to get through the session which, itself, was comparatively easy. It was the setting I disliked, the clinic itself: I felt so trapped. This was no good. I couldn't imagine a month of high anxiety. I became discouraged and disillusioned. I soon doubted the lasting effect of Bob's prayer and was sure that God had deserted me again. I obviously expected Him to watch over me and look after me with no effort or acknowledgement on my part. I contemplated not returning to the group.

When Wednesday evening rolled around I did go. This time there were a few new faces, and some familiar ones from the previous week. It felt like being at home in a way. The genuine feelings of warmth and friendliness were there. Some people were dressed in housecoats and slippers; others were covered with blankets because they were not feeling well. The fortunate ones like me were dressed in everyday attire.

Bob started the evening by asking if he could say a special prayer for Brenda. We all agreed, even though the new people had never met her. Bob prayed that God would take her soon. That she was ready to be with Him. What a shock! Brenda was ready to die! She had been told that there was no more that could be done for her. Some of us were amazed. She was so calm at the last group and was happy to be "going home." We were under the impression that "home" meant her house, but she meant she was going to be with God. The group was sober for a few minutes but after a discussion of how happy she seemed and how she would no longer have to suffer we all decided to be happy for her.

How Cancer Saved my Life – I Spy God!

Brenda was not afraid to die; she was ready to be with God. What an inspiration this was. I admired her strong faith. During my stay at The Lodge I met others who were sent home with no hope. It was heart wrenching to witness their torment and that of their loved ones. My personal gratitude kept increasing by leaps and bounds.

Bob did his trip around the group asking for names and information. When my turn came I told them all about my positive experience of the first appointment. How I had recalled Bob's prayer and had calmed down. Everyone was happy to hear this piece of news. On the second sweep, Bob asked for worries and concerns. "Mary the Cynic" was more than ready to air hers! "Why was I so darned anxious in that building? Every time I go in there I become a quivering mess. Where was God when I really needed Him?" Someone asked me if I had prayed for myself en route. I had to admit that I hadn't and that it really hadn't crossed my mind to do so. I felt rather foolish. But I was far too busy being anxious, thank you very much! In my mind praying was still reserved for extra-large desperation. When it was time for Bob to say his individual prayers he again asked God to watch over me when I was in the clinic. I must admit I received a feeling of delight at having a prayer said just for me once more. It was time to sing the hymn, "Safe in the Shadows of the Lord." I didn't feel the least bit silly this time. In fact I had looked forward to it:

> *From fears and phantoms of the night,*
> *From foes about my way,*
> *I trust in Him, I trust in Him,*
> *By darkness as by day.*

The same thing happened as before. I felt the tears well up again and I felt God's presence. I didn't tell a soul.

Over the next week I struggled through my daily trips to the clinic. Some days were easier than others were but they were all far from perfect. The anxiety still plagued me. I did remember to say a little prayer sometimes, but they were just little ones compared to Bob's. I really was becoming disillusioned again. Bob's big prayer was helping but somehow it was not enough. I needed more clout.

I wanted this to be a spiritual journey, a healing of my soul as well as my body. The funny thing was that I wasn't too concerned about my body because my prognosis was so good. But I was nowhere near Brenda or Lucy's level of faith, I was afraid to die and not too timid to admit it.

Over the course of the week I thought long and hard about what had and had not happened. I felt God had heard and responded to Bob's prayers on my behalf, that it had taken a perfect stranger to suggest that I say a prayer for myself! When I did attempt to pray they were just little prayers that lacked luster. They resembled damp firecrackers, not much fizz! It was then that I decided to pluck up the courage and ask Bob if I could have an hour of his time. I was in need of some spiritual guidance. He told us all that he was available for individual counseling if we felt the need.

When I approached Bob with my request he was more than happy to oblige and we arranged an appointment time then and there. I would be seeing him before the next group, which was what I had hoped. It was important, as my time was going by quickly now and my treatment would soon be finished. I had to get this spiritual stuff right. I was getting anxious as I needed some answers to many questions and I certainly was confused.

Mary Jane Warr

Mary Jane Warr

6
LETTING GOD IN

Listen! I am standing at the door knocking; if you hear my voice and open the door, I will come in to you and eat with you and you with me.

Rev 3: 20

I met Bob in the chaplain's office; it was a peaceful and comfortable meeting place. I found it amazingly easy to relax and started pouring out my doubts and fears. I told him how things just didn't seem to be working out in the prayer department -- I thought God was supposed to answer one's prayers. I told him how wonderful his prayers were and how they had affected me. And yes, the hymn! I went on to say that, at times, I felt that God had deserted me, rejected and abandoned me just as other significant people in my life had done previously. I felt insignificant, like a mere speck in the universe, and not worthy of His time and effort, forgotten and ignored. I admitted that I felt that God didn't love me and that, somehow, He wanted to punish me. I was surprised at the things I was saying. The therapist in me kept screaming, "Low self-esteem."

Bob led me to the topic of trust. He said that he felt that my hang-ups were related to a lack of trust, especially in God. He could understand why I would feel that way. Then we added up the major disappointments and betrayals that I had encountered in my lifetime, many of which I had had to handle alone. I had turned my back on God, as I did not trust Him. For survival, I had become fiercely independent. Bob said if I wanted to feel God's love--and he believed that I really did--then I would have to let those walls down and give God another chance by letting His love in. He explained that God had plenty of love for us all, including me. Bob reminded me of a passage in the bible, Luke 12: 6-7, "Are not five sparrows sold for two copper coins?

And not one of them is forgotten before God. But the very hairs of your head are all numbered. Do not fear therefore, you are of more value than many sparrows." Bob said that if I put my faith and trust in God, all things were possible. God was to be trusted and not feared.

I admitted that asking for God's help was *déjà vu* especially when it came to dealing with anxieties. I was nervous to make another request. As I thought God had rejected and abandoned me I treated Him as though this were true when, in fact, He was there all of the time. He continued to work for me but I was far too busy having a major temper tantrum and being too stubborn and blind to see. It suddenly dawned on me that all I needed to do was to reach out and extend myself to Him.

So I came away from our meeting with the message:

Let your walls down and let God be in your life

Accept that life is unfair at times. If you won't accept this you will become bitter, disillusioned and cynical. Even if the world is unfair, you can still maintain your integrity, your faith and your trust. You have a choice-- to become better or bitter!

Loving God may seem dangerous but it's well worth the risk not to harden your heart and surrender to living an empty life

Be open to love. Risk yourself in the love of God, and you will never be disappointed.

The hour went by all too fast and I thanked Bob for listening to me and for giving me good advice on which to ponder. The trust issue became crystal clear and really made good sense, as did my lack of self-esteem when it came to my relationship with God. I could understand that I was still suffering from a lot of guilt because I had turned my back on Him. I have been through enough personal therapy, and counseled enough people over the years, to understand the importance of trust and guilt and their connection to one's self esteem. In fact, I felt absurd for not having worked this one out myself.

As I left the chaplain's office, Bob suggested that I become involved in a church group, for support, once I returned to Gabriola. I said that I would seriously consider it.

Mary Jane Warr

7
THE POWER OF PRAYER

*God hears no more than the heart speaks:
And if the heart be dumb, God will certainly be deaf.*

Thomas Brooks

Armed with more insight and information, I had the last leg of my treatment to face. The final three radiation sessions would be administered on a different machine, more powerful than the first one, and located at the far end of the hallway. A few zaps of heavy-duty radiation for good luck! These sessions were a week away. That meant one more group meeting before the big machine and the end of my treatment.

At the Wednesday night group I asked for strength and courage to get me through my last week. Bob delivered a "super-prayer" for me and I felt secure. That night our group discussion centered around praying and the power of prayers. Many of us admitted that we had several kind people praying for us while we were undergoing our tests and treatments. We agreed that just the thought of all of those prayers being said on our behalf certainly had a huge impact. When we took a good look at praying many of us confessed that we didn't really know where to begin. We had put God on a pedestal and we felt small and insignificant before Him. We were lost for the appropriate words.

It was determined that when we pray we have a personal conversation with God. Prayer is worship and a solemn practice of thanksgiving; it is a time when we can present our earnest requests to God. Prayer is reverence and respect paid to God. Through prayers we can embrace the reality of God's presence. If we confide in Him, He will help us. Prayer is not about trying to sound holy or humble enough to get God to listen. God doesn't want us to put on a show: acting or sounding as who we think He wants us to be. We don't have to manipulate, neither should we pay lip service. God wants us to come to Him in an honest, natural way. Yes, He is God, and we should approach Him with the deep respect and honor that He so greatly deserves.

Prayer can have powerful physiological effects on the body. Used as an expression of spirituality, prayers can work in concert with medical treatment to bring about physiological changes and recoveries. Prayer can be a great stress reliever. In the bible, prayer is often used to vent anger to God. It isn't always good to express anger freely to people, yet we have to release our feelings. Prayer is a great way to do that. Speaking the words, even in a whisper, has a greater release for me than saying them in my mind or head. It allows me to concentrate better. Prayer time is my private time, which I look forward to each day. Sometimes I will say a prayer quietly in my mind, depending on the situation. Telling God honestly how we feel and opening up to Him is the beginning of healing. It is said that He is the greatest heart specialist in the universe!

There are times when just listening to our own prayers makes us feel better. It is a form of soul searching and problem solving.

Ralph Waldo Emerson said, "No man ever prayed heartily without learning something." Prayer offers us a time for reflection.

I told Bob in front of the group that his prayers had really been an inspiration and a great help; that he was a "natural", and could we please have his secret! He said it was perfectly okay to talk with God as though He was sitting right in front of us. We could converse with Him as though we were talking to our best friend. He wouldn't mind one bit if we poured our heart out to Him. Bob guaranteed that God would listen. He said that if the thought overwhelmed us we should start small.

He related a story of two widows who were great friends. Both had lost their husbands within a short time of one another so these women clung to each other for support and company. They would phone or visit each other daily. As they worked their way through their grief they decided that the time had come for them to stop feeling sorry for themselves and to turn their negativity into something more positive. Instead of wallowing in their losses they decided to start seeing the good in things around them. They invented the game of, "I spy God!" Each evening they would talk on the phone and relate all of the good things they had experienced that day. It could be as simple as "I saw my first snowdrop this morning. I spy God!" Or, "I received a letter from my granddaughter today. I spy God!" Any small event was noted and they each praised God at the end of the day for these tender mercies.

"Mary the Cynic" had another question for Bob. "How can I be sure that God will listen to my prayers. He let me down before. How could I trust that He would listen?" Bob said that God did indeed listen to all prayers. Sometimes our prayers aren't necessarily answered in the way we anticipate or expect. It is important to remember that our prayers and requests are answered and sometimes in ways that are even bigger and better than we expected. God is love. If He doesn't answer our prayers in a reasonable length of time we have to realize that God has His reasons and that He is probably busy making other arrangements or plans for us that will prove to be much better for us in the long run. Bob reminded us that:

- God always has our best interests at heart
- He is a loving God who reveres us
- We are all God's children and He cherishes each and every one of us in a very special way.

I realized that I needed to change my attitude and start thinking about God in a whole new light. Instead of defying and challenging Him, because of my fear and ignorance, I needed to see Him in a loving and positive way. I could see clearly that fear and mistrust had been my stumbling blocks. I was now better equipped and more confident to start praying for myself. And how I prayed! As I entered the clinic I asked God to please be with me and not to leave my side until I exited the building! Amazingly, each time a calm came over me. I walked serenely through the building as cool as a cucumber. I knew God was with me. He had heard my prayers and was right beside me. Oh, what a feeling! Each day it was the same. I began to look forward to stepping inside the main doors of the clinic. I was putting my faith and trust in God not to let me down and He didn't. When it came time for the final three treatments my prayers were definitely answered. I couldn't believe the change in my behavior and attitude. I was now acting my age and not behaving like a frightened, defiant little child any more. It felt so good. The three "big" radiation treatments were a breeze. He filled me with the strength and courage that I needed. I spy God!

A transition had taken place. When it came to God, "Mary the Cynic" no longer existed, she had finally seen the light. God never left her; it was she who had turned her back on Him. I felt like Scrooge, when he discovered the Spirit of Christmas in "A Christmas Carol". He said, "I haven't lost my senses, I've finally come to them!" Now I could see.

This would be my last group night. Tomorrow was my final treatment and then I was free to go home for good. I was elated to share all of my news but sad to say goodbye to my new friends. This group, ever changing though it was, certainly had worked wonders for me.

Bob did his usual trip around the circle and when it came time for my prayer request I blubbered like a baby. I surprised myself. This was to be my last prayer from him. My heart was so full of gratitude and relief. I was grateful to be alive and relieved to be going home to my family and Gabriola.

I shall be eternally grateful to the doctors, nurses and technicians who, with God's help, healed my body. I was grateful to The Lodge staff, for their tender loving care, and for my roommate Lucy who was such a sweetheart. I was certainly thankful and appreciative of dear Bob, my Messenger Angel, who I am convinced God put in my path. And the Wednesday night group members, who had offered love and support so willingly all of the way through my journey. I was certainly going to miss them. Most of all, I was grateful to God for orchestrating the whole thing and for watching over me.

We sang:

> *Safe in the Shadows of the Lord*
> *Possessed by love divine,*
> *I trust in Him, I trust in Him,*
> *And meet His love with mine.*

When it came to the trust bit I sang those words with conviction. I decided then and there that by trusting God I had nothing to lose but everything to gain.

CONVERSATION

Don't let the word "prayer" frighten you "Prayer" is just the word people use when they talk about communicating with God.

- Prayer is not a formal, mysterious ritual.
- It is simply conversation between God and his children.
- It should be as natural as talking to a friend on the phone.
- God is interested in you.
- Your feelings and worries, great or small are significant to Him:
- that bill you can't pay,
- the sunrise you enjoyed so much, your upcoming annual review.
- He cares about it all.

You don't have to ask for a grand, miraculous display of power every time you pray.

And you don't have to try to impress God. Just make your specific, down-to-earth requests and discuss your common, human feelings.

All you have to do is talk.

(Anon.)

Mary Jane Warr

8
BLESSINGS IN DISGUISE

Gratitude is one of the least articulate emotions, especially when it is deep.

Felix Frankfurter

My daily prayers have formed a pattern of their own with much gratitude, appreciation, thanksgiving and requests. It took me a while to understand that it was okay to ask for things that were important to me. I am now truly convinced that God does listen to our prayers and answers them in His own way. In fact, at times I am amazed at the speed with which some of my prayers are answered. There is no doubt in my mind that God does exist and my belief that this is so is intensified at these times. He is constantly watching over me. I often feel overwhelmed by the many blessings that He sends my way.

Have you ever felt that you can't believe that an all-powerful and all loving deity would allow so much sorrow and destruction in His world? I have, and I know that this thought has crossed many people's minds. We even sometimes refer to natural disasters as "an act of God." Why would God allow atrocities like wars, violence, murder, cruelty, acts of terrorism, earthquakes, volcanic eruptions, storms, floods, droughts, famine, disease to occur if He is indeed a kind and loving God?

Why is it that when tragedy does strike, like a car or plane crash, some people die instantly, others are badly maimed or injured, while others can walk away physically unscathed? Theologians and philosophers have been trying to answer these questions for centuries and to this day I don't think they have been able to come up with any clear answers. As soon as something bad happens, people want to blame Satan or the Devil for these acts, not wanting to believe that God could possibly do anything that would harm any living thing that He had created. I don't believe there is any such thing as "evil." It is simply ignorance gone to the bad.

God has to use "tough love" sometimes. When bad things happen I have to remind myself that there is always a reason. I may not like the things that happened, they may sadden me, but I decided long ago to accept the premise that we are not supposed to know or understand everything; that God does work in mysterious ways, some of which make no sense to us at all. I believe that God does have His master plan not only for you and me as individuals but also for the whole universe as well. Everything fits closely together and dovetails somewhere along the way. Forest rangers, for instance, say that while forest fires are dangerous, frightening and certainly destructive, they are also necessary once in a while so the forest can have a chance to revitalize and refresh itself. Forests grow old and outgrow themselves or become too thick and dense for healthy growth. They tend to see forest fires as an act of cleansing. They can be astounded at how quickly the forest will rejuvenate itself after a fire, a process that commences immediately afterwards. New green shoots appear among the charred debris and the wildlife soon returns in full force.

I wish there was a way we could stop dreadful things from happening, but I spy God! All I can do as an individual is to pray. I do pray earnestly for peace, for those in despair and in need. I pray for rain for those who desperately need it and for the rain to stop where there is too much. I pray for help for those with diseases and so on. Yes, I can send money to relief agencies and other worthy causes, and certainly each penny helps, but money will not stop these things from happening. We cannot interfere with God's plan and must trust that He does know exactly what He is doing.

On occasion life does seem unfair. Others appear to get ahead while we are left behind. They seem to have everything their hearts desire and you don't; things seem to fall into place for them while you struggle for your very existence. Prayers are not about instant gratification. As I mentioned earlier, sometimes you have to pray hard for what you want or need. There are times when answers are delayed or are not forthcoming. But what I think I want, and what God knows is best and right for me, can be two different things.

Sometimes He makes us work hard for things, either to test our faith and true belief or so that we will appreciate the end result. Nothing truly happens by chance.

Sometimes, it may seem as if we are being forced in a direction we don't want to go. Over the years I can see how stubborn and persistent I have been. If my mind was set on something, I would work it from all angles until eventually I would surrender, exhausted and defeated, putting myself through a lot of stress, worry and hard work only to emerge disappointed and frustrated. That was before I was clued-in to God's plan for me. When things don't work out maybe we are going against His Will. We may not always like or appreciate what He has in mind for us. God is at work in our lives even when we don't recognize or understand it. A friend of mine once said, "Beware of substituting your own wishes for God's Will." It is easy to become discouraged but it is wise to remember that God is LOVE and that He does have our best interests at heart. Remember the saying; "Be careful what you ask for because you may get it!" I am sure at times that there are some things we are not supposed to know or understand.

These are the mysteries of life. William Cowper, an English Poet, wrote:

> *God moves in a mysterious way*
> *His wonders to perform;*
> *He plants his footsteps in the sea,*
> *And rides upon the storm.*
> *Blind unbelief is sure to err,*
> *And scan his work in vain;*
> *God is his own interpreter,*
> *And he will make it plain.*

I thank God for His tolerance and patience. I must really have made Him shake His head at times. He may even have got a chuckle out of my persistent antics. I have learned my lessons well.

How Cancer Saved my Life – I Spy God!

My request to go to a private school was not answered. I was put out but when I really think about it I understand that the life experiences of going to a regular senior school helped mold my character and prepare me for the real world. I needed to come out of my shell. Senior school was a place of survival of the fittest and I became a survivor. I still think I would have loved private school! But I cannot argue, God does know best.

When I fell to my knees in desperation, I wouldn't have gained the much needed knowledge and insight if God had taken away my panic attacks. I wouldn't have had the golden opportunities that came my way because of my panic disorder, which included meeting and talking with hundreds of dear people who have crossed my path as a result. My personal understanding of fears, phobias and anxieties have been a blessing in disguise. I have had twenty-five wonderful years working as a counselor and therapist, helping others with these and similar maladies, a job I loved. God did answer my prayers in His own time and in His own way. He had me learn just about everything connected to panic disorder so that I could help others. And he gave me Ernie!

My cancer journey taught me many things, some of which I have shared with you. I think one of the best was to understand and appreciate God's patience. He watched "Mary the Cynic" wrestle and tussle with life, determined to tough it out without His help. It took a mighty big scare, a club on the head, to make me see that life is richer, fuller and so much easier and far sweeter with Him fully in it. I thank Him for His patience, tolerance and understanding. It isn't until you acknowledge God's presence that you feel truly loved and blessed. We don't have to wait for a tragedy or a bolt of lightning to give us a wake-up call. We can get in touch with Him at any time and start a lifelong mutually loving relationship. He is very happy when we come to Him willingly. It's easy, just start by making a note of every good thing that happens to you and make a point of thanking God daily, in your own way, for His tender mercies. It is never too late to begin. He is waiting for you to approach Him. "Mary the Cynic" used to scoff at people who claimed they had seen the light. I can hear her say to herself, "Oh yes, right!" But that was before it happened to her, that is why "The Cynic" no longer exists. At times just to say "thank you" doesn't seem enough.

Gratitude is difficult to express in terms of depth of feelings.

Mary Jane Warr

Mary Jane Warr

9
STOP, LOOK AND LISTEN!

Let observation with extensive view,
Survey mankind from China to Peru;
Remark each anxious toil, each eager strife,
And watch the busy scenes of crowded life
                                        Vanity of Human Wishes

I left Vancouver a different person, much happier and far more grateful. Finally I had begun to let God into my heart and I was truly thankful for the journey.

There are times when I am sure God tests our faith and trust in Him. Some people say, "God never speaks to me!" God does speak to those who take the time to listen.

Sometimes he speaks to us quietly, almost subliminally, while at other times He is quite blatant. He wants to talk to us but we are often too busy, stubborn or preoccupied to listen. If we took more time it could make life much easier. I can give you a prime example.

Today, as I write this, it is Monday of the August long weekend. This morning, Brandy and I took our usual walk, which included a stop at the local mini-market to get a newspaper for Ernie. Some holidays the paper is delivered to the island but not others, so it was anyone's guess as to whether we'd be lucky and find one today. The weather was threatening when we left home. I decided not to take my backpack and wallet, instead I grabbed my umbrella and put a dollar in my raincoat pocket. The paper is usually eighty cents on weekdays. When we arrived at the mini-market there was a small pile of newspapers there, which is unusual. There is usually a large pile first thing in the morning. I quickly picked one up and stood in line, as the little store was becoming full of people. When I arrived at the counter I laid my dollar down on the counter. The clerk, who was new to me, scanned the newspaper. "That will be $1.87," she said. I looked at my dollar and then at the paper. I was truly surprised. I asked her why the paper was extra today as it was Monday! "It's a holiday special," she said. I must have looked a bit stunned. "A holiday special!" I replied, in disbelief. "I only have a dollar, I thought it was eighty cents today." Again she replied, "It's a holiday special and it costs $1.87". I asked her if I could take the paper and pay her the eighty-seven cents the next day when I came by. She said, "No. I'm sorry, I can't do that." I was now very aware of the lineup behind me. Not one to let things rest, my eyes darted around to the back of the store to see if I could spot a familiar face. I know most of the staff members and I knew they would trust me for eighty-seven cents until tomorrow, but there was no other help in the store. The clerk was alone. I asked her politely to please save a paper for me and that I would return with the correct amount.

Brandy and I continued on our walk and as we did so I was having a pout. After much gnashing of teeth I began to work things out:

- First, I was not embarrassed by what had happened, and that was good

- Second, the sales clerk was doing her job. She didn't know me so why should she break the rules?

- Third, I assumed the paper would be eighty cents, not even thinking there would be a holiday special

- Fourth, it meant that once I arrived home I would have to jump in the car and drive all the way back to the store again – what a bother!

After relating my tale of woe to Ernie, I jumped into the car, with my wallet this time, and drove to the store to collect the paper. When I arrived home, I glanced at the headlines and they looked familiar. I looked again. Oh no, we already had one of these. This was Saturday's weekend paper, which the clerk had referred to as "the holiday special!" I was beginning to feel pretty ridiculous. No wonder there was only a small pile of papers in the store so early in the morning; and the weekend edition is always $1.60 plus tax. Why didn't I clue in? It served me right for not paying attention. There was no Monday paper due to the holiday.

The way I chose to see this situation was that God was quietly telling me not to buy the paper. He was whispering in my ear, "Can't you see there is something wrong here?" Or, "Why don't you question what the holiday special is?" I left the house with a dollar only, which is unusual. Why did I decide to do that? Once in the store I noticed only a small pile of papers. He was trying to tell me something here but I didn't pay attention. Then there was the cost, $1.87 that I didn't have, another clue. Yet I continued on without stopping to look and listen. I let God's message go right over my head, again! He let me finish my transaction only to show me how stubborn I had been. If I had listened to Him I could not only have saved myself precious time and the frustration, but also the $1.87! A small example but a meaningful one, I think.

How many times have I not listened to God, or been unobservant of His intuitive clues, that I have chosen to ignore. As a blatant message, I have another really good example.

One of the details that really attracted me to our country home was the wonderful soaker tub in the bathroom. It is big, long and deep, with an invitingly comfortable shape to it. There is nothing I enjoy more than filling the tub with hot water and bath beads and then soaking in the sweet smelling water up to my ears. My Piscean personality may have something to do with my love of water; I find it soothing. Soaking in the tub is a particularly good time to daydream, problem-solve, or to just let my thoughts run wild. I call it my "think tank". On occasion, as I release the water after my bath, I may send an affirmation with it, such as "I let go of all tension in my body", as I watch the water swirl down the drain. Another time it may be, "I discharge the pain from my left big toe." It really has become more of a game that I play than anything else. One day, after pondering on how very negative my thoughts can become at times, I pulled the plug and said, "All negative thoughts,

GO!" Symbolically, I flushed them down the drain and it felt so good as they started to swirl away.

Once out of the bathtub I happened to glance back and noticed that the water had not emptied completely. It was draining away very, very slowly from the tub. I didn't think too much about it and went on my merry way. Later, after using the toilet I noticed the same thing was happening, the water was taking it's time emptying. Then I looked at the tub. A black, gooey substance was bubbling up from the drain, how unpleasant! I called for Ernie's help. We tried the plumber's helper, the plunger, but no results. Next we tried pouring boiling water down the drain but it just regurgitated more of the black gooey stuff, more aggressively this time. When the dishwasher, way off in the kitchen, began to empty itself the result was like Old Faithful. This was a big problem, much bigger than my very handy husband could fix.

It was time for action, so we called the plumber, who was most helpful over the phone. He told Ernie to check various things. He seemed to think that the difficulty was in the septic tank, a blockage of some kind. He instructed Ernie to dig out the opening of the tank to see if there was any movement or water flow. If the water was not moving, it was most likely blocked and could be freed easily by pushing a stick or rod into the entrance pipe. Lucky Ernie! Well, this was indeed the problem. It was easily fixed at no expense, thanks to our friendly plumber, and Ernie's muscle power and good nature.

After things had returned to normal and the household water flowed beautifully like the Athabasca River, I confessed to Ernie what I had done. How I had told my negativity to get lost. Wow, I didn't realize there was so much! We really had a good laugh over this one. But when I stopped and really thought about it I'm sure that God was at work. While I have tried to remain optimistic throughout my life there has always been an underlying negativity within me. It was something I couldn't seem to shake. This experience certainly did the trick. I must say that since this disgusting backup occurred in my beautiful think tank I have been cured of negativity. I haven't allowed myself a negative thought since. I thank God for attracting my attention in a very obvious way. This blatant approach has really worked wonders.

Today I have made a pact with myself to be more observant and in tune with God. To stop, look and listen. If I am in line with His Will I know things will go right for me.

Mary Jane Warr

10

PLUGGED IN!

There is only one religion,
though there are a hundred versions of it.
George Bernard Shaw.

It was wonderful to be home. I felt so well and free. My nightmare was behind me and I had come through intact. I spy God! The summer was the best, the fresh island produce tasted sweeter and juicier than ever. It was a picture postcard summer and the sun stayed with us well into fall. Music was sweet sounding like never before. All was right in my world.

I often visited my special place and lifted up my eyes to "those" hills and I found myself openly talking with God. I played, "I spy God", and would thank Him for the things that I was beginning to see and appreciate around me: each beautiful day, the eagles circling overhead, the magnificent view, the warm sunshine. All of the good things that had happened in the past twenty-four hours, no matter how trivial; I felt that if I had noticed them, then they were worth mentioning. I didn't want to miss a thing or to take anything for granted. I was beginning to see God in everything; the things we see, touch, taste, and smell. He is everywhere and in everything we do.

I did not attach myself to a church as Bob had suggested. If I did join a church I really didn't know which one I would choose as I was still confused about religion and spirituality, and this was part of my quest. I was beginning to see "religion" as formal and organized, and "spirituality" as informal, even though they are one and the same. I must admit that I was far more comfortable with the latter. To me, spirituality is a free association with God, independent religion via the soul.

I still felt the need to sort things out on my own, with God's help of course. I did share some of my journey with a friend of mine who is a religious person. She asked me how I was going to keep my faith strong if I didn't attend church or a spiritual group of some kind. At that time I wasn't sure but I find more and more that God does put the right things in front of us at the right time, if our eyes are open to seeing them.

Over the years I have never slept well. On those nights when I just couldn't sleep, I had found that a portable radio with headphones helped me to remain calm if I should wake up in the middle of the night. I just "plugged in." I learned to be selective, not listening to anything that would set the adrenaline in motion like bouncy music or aggressive phone-in shows. One night, quite by accident, (or was it? I am learning that nothing is by accident), I stumbled upon a religious station. The person speaking was talking all about God and His love. He wasn't a bible-thumping, holier-than-thou type of person, but someone with a friendly, calming and reassuring voice that offered solace, understanding and good old common sense. Like Bob, he was my kind of theologian. This was a first for me, "Mary the Cynic" was actually listening to religious radio. He held my interest and attention. It was comforting and at the same time reassuring to me that I was indeed on the right track. This person was speaking my language. It was as though God had plugged me in on purpose.

That radio station houses many ministries. Each has its own mission and focus for promoting God's work. They also have their own host personalities. But the message is the same, to spread the word that God is good and, indeed, LOVE. That He is life itself. That every living thing comes from Him and that He loves us all because we are His own.

To some, this newly found knowledge may seem basic but it's amazing how one can stumble through life without having a clear understanding of the most fundamental things. I learned so much about religion and spirituality by listening and then thinking things through. I must admit not all dogma or every doctrine was for me, but I have learned to be selective without feeling guilty. Quite a few of these faceless people became my mentors and friends, helping me to rediscover God at a much deeper level.

I think we can all relate to the fact that when we are ready to accept something new, information seems to come to us through various channels or sources. The book that you are looking for seems to fly off the shelf at you; articles of interest appear in magazines or the newspaper; television shows or movies seem to have a special message just for you because you're open to a new or different concept. When we are vulnerable things certainly seem to have more impact.

One night I noticed that my mind was wandering. The person talking was obviously not holding my attention so I was tuning him out. It was then that I took off my rose-colored glasses and I unplugged. The messages were becoming so repetitious. I realized that this station had served its purpose. I had gleaned the pertinent information, which had now cemented in my mind. I shall always be grateful for the experience. It was then that I began to see the radio station as more of a marketing tool. As I mentioned earlier, each ministry had its own mission or focus and each was desperate for funds. Every twenty minutes or so listeners were bombarded with pleas for donations, "love gifts," or ways in which you could purchase the most recent or pertinent books and tapes they had produced. Somehow I didn't like the idea of packaging and marketing God. I decided to put my skepticism away and chose to see that these people are sincere in what they do and how they do it. The station is relatively free of commercials so the programs have to be funded somehow, as do the missionary field trips to faraway places. I reminded myself that God does know what He is doing. I gave myself some gold stars for my change in attitude. My sleep has improved tremendously as I am far more relaxed and content. But we all get the occasional bad night. On those nights I'm glad to plug in and visit my old friends but now I am even more discriminating. I realize I really "struck gold" the first time that I plugged in. I am even more convinced my friend was put there just for me.

Mary Jane Warr

11

THE BIG PICTURE

I shall light a candle of understanding in your heart, which shall not be put out.
   Apocrypha 1 Esdras. 25:14

One of my biggest "radio revelations" had to do with guilt. Even through all the personal therapy addressing self-esteem and forgiveness, I had never really rid myself of the last traces of resentment and guilt. I always seemed to be battling my guilty conscience, often for the most ridiculous things. No doubt I was left with a large guilt complex. In fact, I almost accepted that this was "just me" or "just life" and that I would eventually get used to it. This notion never really satisfied me. I think I always understood the moral code. If I had done something wrong, had "sinned", as soon as I admitted it to myself my honesty would be good enough for God. He would forgive me immediately. It was forgiving myself that was the problem

   It all came together while listening to a religious program on the radio. The pastor was talking about forgiveness and God's mercy. He went on to say that God can forgive us because He loves us passionately and with the purity of unconditional love. Importantly, He understands our "big picture." He knows everything there is to know about each and every one of us, even down to the number of hairs each individual has on his head. As He knows us inside out and upside down, we do not have to explain ourselves to Him. This new information was exciting to me. He knows why we act and react to things the way we do by taking all of our personal history into account. It all became perfectly clear. I do not have to explain myself to God, or justify my position, or become defensive. He understands me implicitly, completely and without question. Because of this, He is not judgmental; there is no need for Him to be. He understands and loves me just the way I am in spite of it all, and because of it all. This information put a very large piece of my puzzle together. It provided me with answers to many of my questions and comfort to many of my personal concerns.

I realized that each of us has a "big picture" that explains every detail of our life that is etched in place. Each circumstance is a part of God's plan and each event is helping to produce who I am. I see my big picture as a collage or mosaic of my life's experiences that blend one into another, glued together, often with fear from the past.

Life becomes interesting when we interact with others. Each of us reacts the way we do because of our past history. Whether our behavior is appropriate or inappropriate will depend on our big picture. Our individual collages briefly merge one with the other, creating yet another part of our own big picture. Some blend and are compatible and beautiful while others clash and become harsh and ugly. Each inter-action becomes another life experience. Whether positive or negative, they affect the way we deal with life and with others in the future. The big picture continues to grow with age and experience.

Another way of seeing one's big picture is to visualize it as a colorful personal handbook or journal, which holds your life story between its covers. It is in-complete until our ultimate demise. We all have a "big picture" and we all have personal history, and stories to tell about ourselves, and what makes us tick. It pays to realize this so that with each inter- action, we can take the whole person into account especially when we find ourselves wanting, or worse still, being judgmental. Consider that the average person has had only a glimpse of this collage. It is hardly fair to judge someone based on just a brief look. If we do not share much, or any, of our big picture with others then they are left to assume, or suppose, that they are right about us, that they know and understand us, and will treat us accordingly. The old cliché, "Never judge a book by its cover," really says it all.

This new concept was so freeing. I had spent much of my life trying to explain myself to people, to justify my position, or by becoming defensive just to survive and protect myself. They didn't seem to know or understand me, or my needs. Come to think of it I was not encouraged to voice my opinions on very much but was expected to go along with what everyone else wanted and expected of me. For safety's sake I became a people-pleasing person. I found this existence frustrating, painful, humiliating and exhausting at times. It became apparent that as I tried to please everybody there was always somebody who didn't like it. I was spending too much time and energy explaining to others what I was going to do, and why, or why I did what I did. I did not believe in myself.

It was wonderful to discover that it is so comfortable and easy to be myself with God, as there is no need to explain anything to Him. He knows and understands the real me and I love Him dearly for that. I have also learned that if you believe in yourself, explanations are unnecessary. Just get on and do what you know to be right for you.

I finally figured out that in order to let go of my guilt I needed to treat myself as God does. To love me absolutely and unconditionally with the understanding that every move, motion, thought, emotion, action and reaction I make are all based on a collection of past experiences: my personal history, my big picture. I am not a bad person because of any of it. On the contrary, everything that has happened to me has been circumstantial and a part of God's plan for me. I thank God for my life's experiences.

As I was loved conditionally by most of the important people in my life I had learned to do the same thing. Only I took it one step further. I could not love me or allow others to try to love me, until everything I did was perfect and good enough. There was no room for faults at all. This revelation told me a lot about my self-esteem or, rather, the lack of it. I had come to expect that people would criticize or judge me if I made a mistake, large or small, and anticipated their criticism all of the time. I never felt really lovable or good enough. How could I allow God's love to enter, or anyone else's, for that matter? I was sure His love was conditional too. I learned to approach life cautiously by keeping myself closed. I am happier doing most things alone. Others may see me as cold or aloof but this has been my way of protecting myself from more hurt. Being a loner gave me a sense of freedom. I seldom trust people I do not know, but I can always rely on me. So it seems to me that the reason why people misunderstand God is because they transfer the conditional love of people onto Him. Many of us are much harder on ourselves than God ever would be and we don't give Him a fair chance.

When you realize that God accepts you for who you are you begin to feel secure enough to accept others. Since I have forgiven myself I can forgive those who have hurt me. God's grace helps us to be gracious to others. I can now forgive those who hurt me because they are, or were, in pain themselves. I need to have compassion for anyone who tries to hurt me, for they are truly suffering in their own way. I need to accept others and myself as God's children and not react out of habit but see the spiritual side of any situation. By loving unconditionally and completely I will bear no malice. To finally let go of my remaining guilt and resentments has been wonderful. It has set me free. I thank God for showing me the way, for helping me to understand my big picture. By taking my collage into account I can see that there is no need to keep beating up on myself for past mistakes, experiences or faults. God's love is unconditional. It is unrestricted and absolute. He is not judgmental. It has taken me some time to totally trust this new and different way of being. I thank God each day for loving me for being just who I am, warts and all. Once I saw the big picture clearly, not only was I able to divorce myself quickly from the residue of guilt and resentment but I was better equipped to love others unconditionally too. This really surprised me as I thought I was able to do that well. But a journey to the soul can really make one sit up and take notice and learn to be brutally honest with, and about, one's self.

Mary Jane Warr

12

BODY AND SOUL

*The Lord is my shepherd, I
shall not want,
He makes me lie down in green pastures;
He leads me beside the still waters;
He restores my soul.*
Psalm 23: 1-3

Another "radio revelation" I experienced had to do with my soul. The soul: the spiritual sensitivity of one's personality; the essence of one's being, the moral spirit. Researchers don't know exactly where the soul is situated in the body. They have located all of our physical organs and are beginning to understand the workings of our complex brain. But they cannot locate, or define one's soul, yet they acknowledge its existence and its presence.

I feel sure that my conscience is connected to my soul in some way. When my conscience pricks it's as though God is letting me know what is right and wrong in any situation. When I get the feeling to do or act upon something, or not to, I suspect it is God whispering in my ear.

Before, I didn't really acknowledge my soul, my deep inner being, not in the true sense of the word. I thought we each possessed one but it wasn't until I learned that God actually cherished my soul that the light bulb went on. The fact that God cherished my soul meant that He cherished me too. It was made apparent that God is very proud of all of His souls and loves each and every one. They are the fruits of His labor. This was a powerful and new concept.

I recently discovered a quote by an old sage, which says, "Guard your inner spirit more than any treasure, for it is the source of life." I visualize my soul as being my central core, which houses my instincts and intuition.

Each year when we do our spring planting in the garden, I buy a begonia for a favorite ceramic pot, which sits on our patio table on the back deck. I like to look out of our kitchen window and see the colorful plant enjoying its place of honor, always in awe of its beauty. I am attracted to the bright reds, hot pinks or coral colors and usually choose one of these hues. This year I decided to break with tradition and chose a vivacious buttercup yellow for a change. Despite our unusual cool and dry summer weather the yellow begonia has thrived and been full of blooms non-stop; the yellow heads and dark green leaves complement one another beautifully. God is the ultimate color coordinator and expert! One day I was standing at the kitchen window looking at the begonia and thinking how remarkable it had been and yet, while I appreciated its presence and its beauty, it didn't thrill or delight me in the same way that the red tones of our previous begonias had done. I shared this thought with Ernie. He pondered for a moment and said, "You mean it doesn't touch your soul!" That was it. Right on! He was insightful and correct. While I love yellow as a color, a buttercup yellow begonia just didn't excite my senses. Reds, hot pinks and corals are me, they touch my soul.

All I know is that I need to love and appreciate my own soul. I need to satisfy and nurture it and not my ego. Sometimes we get our ego, (self-pride or self-centeredness), and our soul confused. Without conscious effort one can let one's ego get in the way of one's soul.

To feel passion or strong emotion is acknowledgement that the soul is being nourished. It becomes enthusiastic and alive. The soul is at the very core of our creativity. As in my passion for writing or my passion for long walks with the dog, and so on. I feel intense. These things nurture the spiritual element of my being – my soul. They make me feel fulfilled, happy and content. Being real and true to myself also provides nourishment for my soul. Gone is the wretched emptiness, the aching void. The hole in my soul is now full. My cup runneth over.

I know now that I tried, over the years, to fill the void with things and people. Like buying bigger houses and things to fill them; by travelling to faraway places; trying new jobs and hobbies. I reached out to my husband, my son, my friends, and yes, my clients too, but nothing or no one could fill the place designated by God for Himself. My soul had been neglected for a long, long time. God pushed, poked and prodded from all angles and I am finally waking up and smelling the delicious coffee! I have decided to take time to nourish myself spiritually every day, to nurture the essence of my being, my amazing and beautiful soul. As my soul becomes enriched, I feel complete and rounded; content, loved and fully accepted. I acknowledge that God soothes my soul.

My body is a vehicle for my soul. It complements the essence of my being. It is perfect in its imperfection; it is the flaws that make it unique. God is proud of His work here too and cherishes my body also. I must treat it lovingly and with the respect that it deserves. God not only wants us to respect our bodies but to carefully and lovingly protect them too. My body is God's temple. The way I treat my body is an act of worship in itself. To feel good, to look my best and to take care of myself, without idolizing, is a good thing.

It is important to get adequate and proper rest. I need lots. There are times when the most spiritual thing one can do is to rest. We need rest and renewal in order to live a whole, balanced and complete life. Sleep deprivation is a very real malady in our society today. The Irish have a proverb that says, "The beginning of health is sleep."

There is another saying, "God created you, but He has left the maintenance up to you!" We do have choices. Therefore, I am responsible for taking good care of myself and for acting kindly toward me and on my own behalf. I know what my body needs and I know when something is wrong. It is up to me to act on this knowledge in a loving and caring way.

I thank God every day for giving me my soul. For cherishing it, cleansing it, and for restoring it. I also give daily thanks to God, and praise Him for sparing me and for healing my body.

Mary Jane Warr

13

A TRUE BELIEVER

O taste and see, how gracious the Lord is:
blessed is the man that trusteth in him.
Prayer Book 34:8

The phrase, "Born again" is used by many people who have discovered the truth of a personal relationship with God. They believe they are starting afresh, with a brand new focus. I am much happier, however, stating that I am a "believer." Maybe it has to do with "Mary, the reformed Cynic!" especially since I have been able to clearly see the light. I do believe in God, our Heavenly Father.

To me, the ultimate level of faith is to be able to declare that one is a true believer. Herein lies the secret. A true believer is a person who not only accepts the truth about God, but also trusts Him and His love enough to allow Him to enter their life fully. They have absolute faith in Him and have no doubts whatsoever. As a result they are able to love God totally, with no conditions. If we do this, He will invite us to live in His heart, which is without doubt the most beautiful place to be, offering a sense of belonging. He is pleased if we reciprocate by opening up our own hearts to Him.

The process of becoming a true believer was a real challenge for me as I have always held on to my reins tightly, trying to stay in control of my life no matter what. This need to control has caused me much anxiety and worry over the years due to my lack of faith and mistrust. It isn't easy to give up control if it has become a part of you — in fact the thought can be downright frightening. To make that conscious decision to commit and to surrender all control to God was taking a quantum leap into the unknown, yet the need to commit to Him became very clear. When we commit to God it is an act of belief and trust: to entrust ourselves into His care for safekeeping. Committing to God produces a special feeling unto itself, for which there is no substitute. You can't fake it or make it happen. It leaves one feeling refreshed, cleansed, relieved and unburdened. One feels uncluttered within and totally at peace with oneself. I have learned that the more I surrender myself to God the more freedom I have. I know of people who have become discouraged because they can't get this feeling. It seems illusive and they start to question God and his existence all over again. To commit to God is giving or handing oneself to Him, absolutely and completely. When we do this, when you make your commitment he accepts the package deal enthusiastically, gently and lovingly, because by so doing we have made Him very happy.

A commitment to God requires that we worship Him:

Lovingly and emotionally,

from the bottom of our hearts

Thoughtfully and intellectually

with all of our minds

Passionately and fervently,

from the depths of our souls

Physically and practically,

with all of our strength and with every fiber of our being

Trusting in Him

one hundred percent.

On one of the radio phone-in shows a caller asked, "How do you make that big step to commit?" The host said, "In all honesty I really can't answer that question. All I can say is that you'll know when the time is right. Meanwhile, just focus on God; be aware of Him at all times. Be patient and your turn will come." It reminded me of giving support to clients who wanted to quit smoking or lose weight. I told tell them that they would know when the time is right because it will feel right. If you try to quit smoking or lose weight before you are seriously committed to do so, you are more likely to experience failure and disappointment. It won't work.

I have met many Alcoholics Anonymous members over the years who wrestle with the thought of "let go and let God," which is part of the AA philosophy. It is difficult for them to work through this concept, as there is no concrete way to help anyone to take the quantum leap. If someone is really serious about trying, I still think the radio host gave good advice: "Focus on God, be aware of Him at all times. Be patient and your turn will come." Continue to pray and to give thanks for all things, no matter how large or how small. Play "I Spy God." Recognize God's participation in your life.

Commitment comes to each individual in a unique way. Mine came through a collision of personal trials: the most frightening of which was breast cancer. I could no longer handle things on my own, so I asked for divine intervention and in time it came. God continued to test me on many levels and then one day I declared that I had been fooling myself all along thinking that I was in control and that I could manipulate or alter events and keep things on track. My "control" was an illusion. God has had absolute control all along but He gave me many choices along the way.

The very best choice was to confide and trust in Him. To choose to let Him do the job that pleases Him the most, to watch over me, to love me and to keep me safe and secure. I am committed to God, body and soul. I now have faith in Him at all times to guide me and direct me, to protect me and to love me. I read once that faith is not belief without proof, it is trust without reservation. God is faithful.

In general, trust is a big issue for many people. Sometimes we find it difficult to trust strangers, as we know little or nothing about them. Then, sometimes it is even harder to trust the people we know because we know too much about them! When we trust someone or something it means that we have faith and confidence in them. Actions, rather than words, lead to trust. A lack of trust leads to insecurity and doubt. Trust itself has three components: predictability, dependability and faith, all three of which are necessary for something or someone to be deemed trustworthy. Like respect, trust is earned.

When we feel God has answered our prayers; when He has protected us in some special way, or made His presence felt, our trust increases. If we feel He has somehow let us down as our expectations have not been met, our trust can plummet and we may become suspect and uncertain. Our trust wavers. But to be a true believer, one must trust God implicitly without question, remembering that He does have a definite plan for us. He has given us tools to use and the autonomy to use them. He has also left us with many, many choices. He even gives us ideas and brainwaves. But the end result is that no matter which route we take in life we will eventually arrive at the exact place He has planned for us. We may take a few wrong turns or detours but there are no short cuts! God is the one in control.

A true believer lets God in. It's not easy to give up control, leaving God to do His work in His own way, to trust. It takes courage to let go of the need to control but I highly recommend it, especially for anyone who suffers from fears, phobias or anxieties. He replaces doubt and fear with strength and courage. I have learned that I really have nothing to fear because I know that God is always near; I am safe and secure, protected and sheltered in His love. Knowing and believing that when in God's care there is no need to worry, as He never lets you down, he offers one a feeling of serenity and peace.

Love of any kind is difficult to accept for some people. They feel undeserving of it due to their life experiences. They may be suspicious of a favorable or welcoming reception when it is offered to them, or they may feel uneasy in certain situations:

- When they are being recognized and treated as lovable

- When they are acknowledged in a favorable way

- When they feel truly welcomed by being acknowledged in a genuine way

- When they feel approved of and believed in and are accepted for who they are.

I recently received a great e-mail from my friend Jill after her breast cancer surgery. It read, " I am recovering from surgery, not only physically but emotionally too. I guess that I just didn't want to accept the impact that this would have on me, and thought that, or wanted to believe that, I could just step back into my life like before. This has been a life-altering experience. I have discovered how many people truly love and cherish me and that has been the best thing out of this.

Maybe this had to happen for that reason: for as much therapy that I have had I deep down did not believe it or feel deserving of it. I'm starting to feel it now. It's a foreign feeling, and I'm not always comfortable with it, but I'm getting used to it and I like it. I am beginning to feel genuine entitlement, self-respect and self-acceptance. Wow! Imagine that; most people grow up automatically with those beliefs and never have to struggle to find it for themselves".

What great insight. I know Jill has been searching and searching for these feelings of acceptance. It took cancer to help her see just how lovable she really is. Not only does cancer make you stop and reassess your life; it also helps you to know who your real friends are. It can be quite surprising to see which ones rally around you and show their true colors. The people you thought you could count on, those whom you may have considered to be your real friends sometimes bail out just when you really need their love and support. Perhaps they do truly care, but they do not know how to show it, or they are afraid of doing the wrong thing. Those you had never considered to be good friends may be the ones who come forward with outstretched hands and a warm heart to greet you. There are those who are put off by any kind of religion because they fear it. They may assume that to become a true believer one has to forfeit a part of themselves or their personalities. Not so. True belief in God makes life and living much simpler. The only thing you lose is disbelief. When you think about it, there is no need for dysfunction, and you certainly do not have to become boring or overly serious. I'm certain that God has a wonderful sense of humour and He can see the funny side of life too. In Psalms 118 it says, "It is better to trust in the Lord than to put confidence in man."

Some people misuse religion. Beware of people who use their religion as a front, hiding fearfully behind it. Others say they are devout people and attend church regularly, yet they use religion to impress people because it is the expected or the correct thing to do, especially when trying to obtain a certain social status.

Unfortunately, there are some people who become addicted to religion and are obsessed with it. You may say, "Is that such a bad thing?" Of all the addictions and obsessions there are, I suppose that this one can do the least amount of harm. Personally, I am opposed to people who consider their belief to be the only one, that somehow they are right and those who think differently are wrong, and who insist on forcing their beliefs on to you whether you want them or not.

Some people, too, think they are true believers when, in fact, they are using "blind faith." There is a difference between having blind faith and being a true believer. With blind faith one is careless or even reckless with one's belief system. Take, for example, the person who might step into a high-powered car, not bothering to buckle up their seat belt. They put their foot to the floor and roar down the highway, telling themselves that God will protect them. They feel invulnerable, incapable of making a mistake. It is their method of testing or proving that God will be their guardian, regardless of their impulsive behavior. Blind faith is short sighted.

A great illustration of blind faith came to me on a greeting card. On the front of the card was a picture of a little man sitting on the roof of his house. The house is surrounded by floodwater up to the eaves. The caption read: A man was caught in a flood. Two men came by in a boat to rescue him but he waved them away, shouting, "No, the Lord will save me." One hour later another boat came along but again, the man said, "No, the Lord will save me." Eventually, a helicopter arrived but the man insisted, "The Lord will save me." Unfortunately the man drowned. At the gates of heaven he asks St. Peter, "Why didn't the Lord save me?" St Peter replies, "For crying out loud – he sent two boats and a helicopter, what more do you want?" So much for blind faith.

To be able to trust, you must be willing to take the risk of being trusting.

Mary Jane Warr

14

MY HEAVENLY FATHER

Our Father in heaven,
Hallowed be your name.
Your kingdom come.
Your will be done,
On earth as it is in heaven.
                              Matthew 6: 9 - 10

I must admit I'm a sucker when it comes to weddings; they are usually romantic, beautiful, happy affairs. I even enjoy watching them on the television occasionally. It wasn't until recently I realized that it's not so much the intense loving relationship between the bride and groom that makes me turn to mush, it is the strong bond between certain fathers and their daughters that really turns me into a sentimental fool. They are obviously people who are not afraid to display openly their love for each other. I am fascinated when the father of the bride beams with joy as he gets his first glimpse of his little girl, the apple of his eye, transformed into a real princess for a day. He appears besotted. She may descend a flight of stairs, glowing and radiant with her love, in a dress that is too exquisite to describe. But what really tugs at my heartstrings is when the bride's father is reduced to tears at the very sight of his daughter, or if he lovingly brushes a tear from her eye. Sometimes you watch them as they dance together at the reception and embrace one another, in a special father-daughter loving way. The love in their eyes declares the close bond between them. Hand over the Kleenex please! The mother of the bride usually fusses over her daughter, bursting with pride and adoration. It gives her so much pleasure to see her little girl, now a woman, at her very best. But these female interactions and friendship, warmth and closeness are quite foreign to me. It occurs to me that I am envious of these genuine, precious, loving moments between parent and child. I suddenly feel cheated. I enjoy watching my son interact with his little girls. They are "in love" with one another and it shows. Many children miss out on a close relationship with their parents for various reasons. Loving parent-child unions are based on trust and acceptance as with other intimate relationships. As I mentioned earlier, trust is earned. I read an article recently which suggested that we tend to open up to God the way we are used to approaching our parents or caregivers; that this was particularly true of a father-daughter relationship as well as a father-son bond. As I am not a male person it is difficult to define what a healthy father-son relationship would be. But after having talked to many men over the years their ideals or needs seem to be similar. They do require and expect love, acceptance and security within their primary relationship especially with male figures. They need:

- Support
- Advice
- To be listened to and taken seriously
- To be understood
- To be a comrade or buddy.

That article made a lot of sense. The level of trust between a child and his or her parents can easily be projected onto God.

Even though He is a very busy guy, I now enjoy an exclusive relationship with Him. We are all special to Him, and He has time and energy for each and every one of us. I have learned never to doubt God or His love.

One night when I was "plugged in" on my radio I heard a story that has stuck with me. An Irish parish priest was driving along a country road when he came upon an old drifter sitting on the side of the road with his belongings in a big bag at his side. The priest stopped his car and walked back to where the old man was seated. He looked at the drifter and said, "Could I be giving you a lift into town? It's on me way!" The old man looked up at the priest and said, "Thank you Father, but I'll be just fine. You see, I believe that God is very fond of me." The priest was amused by the old man's comment but appreciated his sentiment. With a tip of his hat the priest left the old man where he was and said, "That He is, you're right. I know you'll be fine. I'll be on my way then."

This story thrilled me. God is very fond of us all and that includes me. How wonderful: I am never alone with God my Heavenly Father, on my side.

> *I believe in one God,*
> *the Father almighty,*
> *maker of all things*
> *visible and invisible.*
>   *The Mass,*
>   *Prayer Book 1662*

Mary Jane Warr

15

HOW CANCER SAVED MY LIFE

> *In a moment,*
> *in the twinkling of an eye,*
> *the trumpet shall sound,*
> *and we shall be changed.*
> *Corinthians 15:52*

There is no doubt in my mind that cancer can be a life enhancing experience. One emerges as a person changed for the better, with a feeling of having been liberated; saved physically and emotionally and, in some cases, spiritually as well. I guess the same can be said of any serious illness or near-death experience, when you are on the "winning" side. You feel you have been spared and given a second chance at life, an opportunity to make changes and better yourself, where the past is forgotten and everything is new.

While I was staying at The Lodge I asked many people what they were planning to change or do differently in their lives as a result of their brush with death. Most were quick and definite with their replies, saying things such as:

I plan to spend more quality time with my family and friends

I will eat healthier meals

I'm going to exercise regularly, no matter what

I've stopped smoking already and plan never to smoke again

To get to know God better

I want to reduce my stress level by working less and playing more

Reduce my weight. I must lose weight

Take better care of myself generally.

Even pamper myself now and then -- I'm worth it

Give up resentment and start forgiving

Let go of my fears and trust more

Enjoy each moment of each day

Look for the good in people.

Be more positive generally

I'm going to stop worrying about things and let life take me where it takes me

Work on my relationship with my partner.

We need to improve our communications

Gratitude! I won't take anything or anyone for granted.

Each day is precious

I want to be more patient and tolerant; less explosive

These were some positive changes, all of which would help these people to live a healthier and happier life. The people who really scared me, and they were in the minority, were those who, when asked the same question replied, "Not a thing. I don't plan to change anything. My life is perfect just the way it is, why would I want to change it?"

I never thought I would be grateful for cancer but the experience changed my life in a very positive way. I discovered that within every difficulty there lies a gift. There is a French proverb that says, "Gratitude is the heart's memory." My gratitude for being spared and for continuing to be cancer-free is ongoing. Not a day goes by that I do not give my thanks to God for cleansing my body. I even thank Him for giving me my wakeup call. It certainly pulled me up short and forced me to stop and think. It's as if I have grown ten feet taller. I realize that I was working far too hard, while avoiding having to face reality. I buried feelings that needed to be addressed. I'm sure God tried to tell me in subtle ways but I was far too busy and didn't listen. So He gave me the BIG one, my greatest dread, to face. It is almost as if He needed to get my attention one way or another.

Life change and transition are often preceded by confusion, by a sense of loss or pain, or by a feeling that things are falling apart. Pain, physical or emotional, can be a wonderful motivator. Pain motivates us to change. Often it is not "seeing the light" that gets us going, but "feeling the heat." Our greatest lessons come from our hurts and pains. We need to regard pain as a catalyst for personal growth. Unfortunately, many of us do not learn the lessons we need to learn until the pain becomes so great that we are forced onto our knees in desperation. Why is pain our greatest teacher? Because when circumstances become bad enough, we are forced to make those necessary changes; sometimes we only learn the value of something – health, money or relationships – by losing it. Every problem has a purpose.

The truth is that we learn more from pain than from pleasure, more from failure than success. Suffering produces our true character. Elbert Hubbard said, "God will not look you over for medals, degrees or diplomas, but for scars." We mature while we journey through the pain of life. On the other hand, everyone gets bumps and scars. It is what we do about them, how we overcome the hurt and the ugliness that, in the end, makes us or breaks us. Some turn to religion, some to the arts, some to helping others, and so on — and some emerge from "scars" with medals, degrees and diplomas that enrich the world.

There is no doubt that He has given me a second chance at life. Maybe this time I will get it right!

Cancer has saved many lives, as well as my own. I spy God!

Mary Jane Warr

16
AN UPDATE

The House

We have been able to put our original, and unattainable, dream home to rest although we are still financially bruised. With special prayers we are just able to hold our own here. With God's help we are beginning to see a light at the end of the tunnel. One day we will be debt free having paid our dues!

The last time we drove past the house it was completed and looked just the way we had envisioned it for ourselves, complete with a red sports car in the circular driveway. There is some solace in knowing that the people who bought it obviously have the same taste or imagination as us. They shared our vision. We sincerely hope they are enjoying their delightful home and that they will be very happy there.

We are still very happy in Grove Cottage, on Gabriola Island, and feel very much at home with the practical station wagon in the long country driveway.

My Special Place

I discovered that this piece of heaven was not mine alone – no surprise! Many people visit it for a quiet moment of reflection or to be inspired by the view. We each respect one another's space and need for those silent, uninterrupted moments in time. But I'm sure that secretly we all wish that it were ours alone. As I write this, my beautiful spot has been sold and the trees clear-cut for an even better view – what a crime! When the lucky purchasers have built their dream home they will truly be living in a heavenly spot.

An Angel called Bob

Bob is now an ordained minister and Pastor of Christ Covenant Church in Leoti, Kansas. I'm sure he will be greatly appreciated by his parishioners.

Bob and his wife Angie, are now the proud parents of three little girls, Diane, and her twin sisters, Rebekah and Julia. These little ones were heaven-sent and the answer to Bob and Angie's personal prayers. I shall always be grateful to Bob for his encouragement and commitment for helping others and me in our time of need. He is, without a doubt, a special gift from God. An angel.

* * * * *

I am happy to say that at present I remain cancer-free and very optimistic about my future. I spy God! My doctor continues to monitor me annually and together we see that I have a yearly mammogram at the hospital. Meanwhile, I do a thorough breast self-examination religiously each month, an absolute must.

And yes, I continue to pray that God sees fit to keep me cancer-free!

Mary Jane Warr

17
IN CLOSING

May God's amazing grace bring comfort to you. I pray that God will always watch over you. That He will protect you, love you and truly bless you!

I will bless you with a future filled with hope, A future of success, not of suffering.

You will turn back to me and ask for help And I will answer your prayers.

You will worship me with all of your heart And I will be with you.

Jeremiah 29: 11 - 13

EPILOGUE

Today, more and more people are being diagnosed with cancer and projections for the future are staggering. According to the B.C. Cancer Foundation, one in three persons can be expected to develop cancer in his or her lifetime.

Cancer touches just about everyone's life in one way or another. If you stop and think about all of the people you know, or have known, who have had to face cancer your list might be quite astonishing. Here is a list of all of the people who have touched my life in some way, people who have crossed my path. Some are family members, others are friends, neighbors and acquaintances. Cancer has no respect for gender, race, age or creed. All of these people have had, or are presently fighting cancer. Some of them have lost their battle.

Alice	Ern	Lynn
Barbara	Gail	Malcolm
Beryl	Hazel	Marg
Betty	Hector	Maria
Bev	Jackie	Marilyn
Bob	Jane	Maureen
Catherine	Jeff	Myra
Chris	Jenifer	Norm
David	Jill	Pam
Denese	Joan	Rhonda
Diane	Joanne	Richard M
Don	Joe	Richard T
Donald	Laura	Roy
Dora	Lawrence	Sue
Einar	Leslie	Vera
Elizabeth	Liz	Veronica
Emma	Lucy	Winnie

My gratitude to:

Ruth: when I said that I would write about my spiritual journey for you, little did I know that it would turn into a book. I thought I could accomplish the exercise in a few pages. Thank you for giving me the inspiration to record my life-altering and very special journey.

I would like to extend my personal and heartfelt gratitude to my prudent surgeon, Dr. Jim Hunter of Nanaimo and Vancouver. Your skills and persistence were my launching pad. I value your gentleness and your humanness, which helped me to feel very comfortable in your care. Thanks also to Dr. Ivo Olivotto and his wonderful team at the B.C. Cancer Agency in Vancouver, whose professionalism was combined with compassion, genuine concern and gentle care. Dr. Olivotto's excellent listening skills were such a bonus – greatly appreciated at such a critical time.

Many people have willingly and generously offered their help, encouragement and support with this book. My grateful thanks to Dr. Marti Cleveland-Innes, Jayne Fagan, Peter Warr and Jenifer Wilson. All donated precious time and expertise reading and critiquing my manuscript. They offered sound advice, insightful comments and plenty of moral support.

The Reverend Bob Everest deserves a special mention for allowing me to write about him. Thank you also to the Reverend Colin Johnstone, retired Chaplain of the B.C. Cancer Agency, Vancouver for his help in locating Bob. My appreciation goes also to the Reverend Walt Brouwer, Pastor of Christ Community Church, Nanaimo, B.C. for giving me permission to use some of his "gems and pearls of wisdom."

A special thank you goes to my agent, Thelma Barer-Stein, PhD., Culture Concepts, Toronto, Ontario, for her excellent suggestions and fine editing skills. She has been a great source of inspiration and support for my writing in general and I thank her for believing in me.

I would also like to express special gratitude to Susan Mellor for bringing her many talents to my rescue at the eleventh hour. Thank you Susan. What would we have done without you? And to the staff at Markham Printing Company Limited: for their patience, excellent work and generosity.

Last, but by no means least, my ongoing thanks to Ernie, my wonderful husband, lifelong partner and very best friend. He was with me throughout my journey and continues to be my greatest advocate. Without him, this book would never have made it to the press. He is definitely my right arm and my better half.

I regard all of the above as heaven-sent. They are no "ordinary" people. I spy God!

ABOUT MARY JANE WARR

Mary Jane Warr received her early education in England. Coming to Canada in 1954, she was taken under the wing of Dr. John S. Jameson, MD, BT., head of the Behaviour Therapy Institute in Toronto. Dr. Jameson became her mentor and friend. Later, she enrolled in the volunteer therapists program at the Lakeview Psychiatric Hospital under the tutelage of Dr. Stephen Neiger, Head of the Behaviour Therapy Unit.

Mary Jane worked as a personal counselor and therapist, specializing in fears, phobias and anxieties. She was the founder and executive director of The Freedom from Fear Foundation in Toronto, Ontario from 1975 to 1979. Later she operated Personal Growth Centre, a treatment and learning facility in Calgary Alberta. Now semi-retired, Mary Jane lives and continues to practice on Vancouver Island, B. C., where she is applying her more than thirty years of experience to the writing of her books.

Mary Warr's self-help books can be seen on her website: http://www.makingsensebooks.ca